HOLLYWATTS

HOLLYWATTS

An Autobiographical Novel by

ARTHUR LAWRENCE CRIBBS, JR.

the pilgrim press

The Pilgrim Press, 1300 East 9th Street
Cleveland, Ohio 44114
thepilgrimpress.com

Published 2023.

Printed on acid-free paper.

Library of Congress Cataloging-in-Publication Data on file.
LCCN: 2023934949

ISBN 978-0-8298-0037-1 (paper)
ISBN 978-0-8298-0038-8 (ebook)

Printed in The United States of America.

ONE

Returning to the intimacy of home on a street formerly familiar, a street now turned vague with houses transformed into tombs possessing the ghosts of stilled voices, is a jarring experience. Remembering what was and used to be stabs a painful, piercing blade into my heart.

Memories conceal the fleeting details of escapades playfully performed by children too innocent to realize the courses their parents had taken. Eventually, each family landed on foreign soil of unbroken earth. Men and women, young and old alike, traveled the dangerous, unmapped roads that snaked across America while executing their planned escapes from too familiar assailants who assaulted their humanity. They refused to be deterred as they successfully and safely arrived on new grounds in search of a better life.

It was not as Dr. Martin Luther King, Jr. poetically and openly dreamt years later while speaking in Washington, DC, on the steps of the Lincoln Memorial. The judgment that pushed my parents and our neighbors from their Southern hometowns to the open frontier of the nation's Pacific Coast was not based "on the content of their character" but "the color of their skin."

These men and women began their journeys in the immediate aftermath of World War II, which fueled determination and inspired courage to migrate from the blood-riddled Southern states of America to the glaring sunlight of Southern California. They arrived in Willowbrook (an unincorporated area of Los Angeles County nestled south of downtown Los Angeles and north of Compton) beaming with pride, hope, and the courage to start anew in a previously distant place. The emerging movie industry presented a kind of utopian appeal to people who desperately sought to escape lynching, public violence, and racial brutality.

Their souls were soothed by going to church on Saturday or Sunday mornings, singing gospel songs, and hearing the uplifting messages proclaimed from pulpits by preachers who had ventured the same course. They carried the bowels of culture and historical episodes deeply lodged in their stretched-tight, darkened skin, which covered steadily pounding hearts pumping blood that flowed through strained veins of worn and weary bodies.

They came to a place in its infancy. It was a modern development designed and constructed almost exclusively for them that included the intricate details to ensure they would not stumble into the wrong neighborhoods of an emerging city that welcomed Midwestern Whites but reluctantly received anyone of African descent.

Our fathers were American warriors who fought battles in Europe, the Philippines, Asia, and places far away from their familiar hometowns. They fought on soil and at sea in places formerly known to them merely as dots on maps. They were survivors whose lives bore the scars of war. They fought for an ungrateful, uncaring nation. Yet, they sacrificed and returned home in search of a better life for themselves and their families.

They had traveled by cars or trains across America from the segregated South. Each one and every family yearned for a paradise where they could thrive, live freely, and make their dreams come true. My parents and our neighbors sought the realization of compatible civility. They brought their visions of hope and desires for opportunities they previously could only imagine were possible. They shared unbridled dedication to make new starts without the limitations so staunchly and constitutionally structured in cities and states where they were born. They simply wanted to live freely and with dignity. They sought a new start and fresh air in the warmth of the bright Los Angeles sunlight.

The sanctioned violence they had known too well back in their hometowns down South seemed null and void.

They arrived with desires to fill an open, free space that lacked the gallows of living trees dangling dead, broken bodies like strange fruit. Their eyes had seen too much on the battlefields of World War II. They knew too well how much America still disdained their existence. It did not matter those Black men had fought and too many had died for a country that resisted their loyalty and denied their humanity.

They had witnessed too many plagues of violence among their distant relatives who were the peoples of the South Pacific, Africa, Asia, and expanses of Europe. Even at home, they could not ignore the decimation of their own Native American cousins and relatives whose ancestors had taken in their great and great-great grandparents and provided protection from a common enemy. Lest they forget the twinned invasion and accompanying assaults on the very tribes that extended hospitality to early European settlers who were often on the verge of starvation after arriving on distant shores and unfamiliar grounds following their crossing of deadly seas. The resulting slaughter and blood of the Seminole, Choctaw, Cherokee, Seneca, and Natchez people course through their veins.

That "Double V" for victory over Nazism and racism that had been flashed on their fingers, pounded in their hearts, and steadied in their heads became more than symbolic for Black families who conspired to help each other realize the promise of a new world. Their optimism to discover freedom without tyranny was etched deeply in the bloody wounds too many suffered and had become too familiar and deeply personal.

So, they came to a land of promise they believed would deliver a better tomorrow with very different episodes than their recent past. They left behind families, friends, and everything familiar to venture onto the seemingly endless highways spanning America that brought them to the neighborhood I would romantically call Hollywatts.

Their journeys had delivered benefits provided by a local Black woman who shared their ambition and foresight. Velma Grant, a real estate agent, looked across the expanse of the rural Southern California landscape and most accurately envisioned a future for what she perceived would be a flood of Black families breaking the color barrier after World War II.

She imagined men—fathers, brothers, uncles, sons, nephews—who had smelled the sweet scent of victory, democracy, integration, and the fresh air of freedom during World War II, and she correctly imagined they would return home in search of a new land for their own families to begin a different life. Her eyes laid sight on a fifty-acre plot that could fulfill the newfound promises of a safe and sane sanctuary for Black people. There she put into place her plans to help them settle and launch their new history.

Velma Grant had a dream in 1945 that required money at a time when the war was winding down and Black warriors were coming back to the United States with grand schemes that needed to be satisfied. She discovered her plan found favor with Bank of America, where she successfully secured a $2.5 million loan to design, develop, and create her black utopia.

Her new homes would be built in the middle of farmlands and horse ranches reminiscent of the Southern landscape quite familiar to her new clients. To make the purchase of these homes even more appealing, Ms. Grant named her housing project after the famous Tuskegee Normal and Industrial Institute educator and scientist who saved both Southern agriculture and the American economy with his discovery of untapped wonders within the peanut and other plants.

Carver Manor, a tract of 250 homes, honored Dr. George Washington Carver and provided affordable housing for the war-weary African American servicemen returning home immediately after World War II.

Situated just south of the Los Angeles city community of Watts, Hollywatts was located in a rural section of Los Angeles County. The arriving veterans settled their families in houses designed by famed African American architect Paul Revere Williams. That magnificent team of Grant and Williams prepared the way for a promised land to emerge. It was on the street where I lived that this story takes place and is told on the following pages.

Long before the promises of security and a future brighter than the evening stars revealed unforeseen opportunities, the strong-minded congregation of strangers would soon become neighbors. Together, they forged paths to realize their desires.

Amid their labor, struggle, and unobstructed visions for their children resided an undetectable menace lurking in the demonic souls of their unnatural enemies, whose warped existence could not bear the idea of Black people having their own untethered achievements.

Beneath the soil and waiting for a more opportune moment were deeply planted devilish seeds that would grow to destroy the unsuspecting Black homeowners and deny them their opportunity to launch a new future. The racist demons had other plans they were determined to deploy from a distance too intimate to detect or deter. The emergence of their scheme signaled a detestable reality that promised to crush the cherished notions of Black warriors, dash their hopes, and eliminate any ideas they had about realizing a professed and promised American dream.

This is an autobiographical novel. Within these pages are the tales that reveal glimpses of the truth about what happened to my community. Names of real people who made the journey in search of a better, brighter life are camouflaged; some characters have had their identities shielded to avoid embarrassment about their actions and the impact they had on my life. This reflective journey guides the reader along the way and moves from house to house, across streets, around corners, and slips into too familiar neighborhoods only separated by the expanse of time and events across the United States.

Life is not linear or bound by continuing episodes. There are intersections with unrelated conditions, circumstances, and climates in places on multiple continents. In search of answers to questions that linger and jingle still, I am striving to understand what happened on the street where I lived that transformed the promised land of my parents and our neighbors into purgatory in a fashion that was beyond their control.

Along the way, I have discovered there have been similar and consistent occurrences that tempted me to fall into a basket of conspiracy theories. Perhaps the actual discovery of such precise instances was merely the result of coincidences. Or perhaps it was something more deeply rooted in a sinister historic pattern that resulted in the demise of cultures and placed restrictions on Black peoples' advancement across America's "land of the free."

Rag-tag street gangs became well-armed, dangerous organizations. Foreign, manufactured street drugs were put into the hands and pockets of little children and desperate adults alike. Guns became readily available and were distributed from the trunks of cars near parks and schools and handed freely to kids like toys. They played with those deadly weapons and achieved the original intent of those demonic souls who delivered them, as live gunfire disrupted tranquility and created battlegrounds for color-coded gangs to thrive, drive-by, and destroy.

For more than five decades, consistent conduct and death-inducing elements devastated communities like mine in a nearly precise scheme, like a plague spreading across America with uniformed destruction bearing the colors, red and blue. Freshly formed gangs split our neighborhood into two divisions of predators whose street families meant more than the natural bloodlines that united them to mother, father, or sibling. The unification of cursory tribes was a new source of belonging, and the induction into street gangs replaced the bonds of inherited genealogy.

During that same period, I witnessed the radical shift in music and lyrics. What were once soulful soundtracks of love, current events, and inspiration for the Civil Rights movement were replaced by a genre identified as

'Gangsta Rap' that was aimed at young Black boys and men. The change was profoundly noticeable and could not be avoided. There was the production and distribution of new music intended to redirect the thoughts, vision, and energy of the youth for the purpose of turning them against each other.

The new musical enterprise was pervasive, effective, and contagious. Motown's love lyrics that dominated Black popular music from the late 1950's began to wane and were ebbed out by violent and vulgar tunes sold from the trunks of cars because they violated Federal Communications Commission rules for broadcast.

The profound shift from wholesome and healthy communities striving toward a brighter day into an unfamiliar new beat echoed across the country with the pulsation of deflated dreams and heralded messages of self-destruction. Love songs were replaced with lyrics that degraded women and bolstered messages of self-hatred and violence perpetrated against neighbors. If the Civil Rights movement produced victories in courts across America, the new vibe and lyrics of self-hatred invaded and pervaded the corridors of Black residents like a plague.

Graveyards and penitentiaries began to fill up, replacing schools and social achievement as previously desired destinations. The demise of our promised land devolved into what is accurately and undeniably purgatory, a place where unfulfilled aspirations reside in a dungeon littered with the remains of the living dead. There is a temptation to deny the reality of such a violent transformation, but the truth must be told and the evidence is too clear to ignore. High school dropouts graduated to armed and dangerous criminals with a destination of prison or premature death.

The unfolding travesty that beset our promised land was replicated in too many places to be coincidence. The shallow shells continue to stand still and preserve a comparative study on the remains of cities like Chicago, Detroit, Oakland, Milwaukee, Gary, Pittsburgh, Cleveland, San Francisco, and Los Angeles. Purgatory is not a distant place of another dimension created as a figment of one's imagination. It is realized in the aftermath of conspiring incidents that define a people's reality and change everything they had hoped to achieve for themselves and their children. It is not the past that is judged; rather, the pitiful future bound by the turbulence intentionally created by outside agents who invaded a land of promise and transformed its existence into an unspeakable arena laced with fear, agony, death, and hopelessness.

The toxic combination of mind-numbing drugs, vile musical lyrics, and the overflowing saturation of handguns and military grade weapons mysteriously placed in the hands of previously unarmed children and youth became commonplace. Violence spread like a virus from coast to coast, community to community, and divided Black people into gangs identified by the colors red and blue.

Fortunately, that is not the end of the story. Rather, we continue to pace toward another passage among the numerous disappointments that resurrected and redirected the results of inhumane conduct intended to deny the humanity of Black people across time and across the United States of America.

In the darkness of midnight on this side of reality, the sun stands at noon where Black people still reside. We may be stunned and stirred awake by the brutal and callous exploitation calculated and executed by treaty breakers, liars, and underdeveloped creatures in human disguise. Those same demons continue to find glory in the diabolical traditions of legalized slavery, lawful abuse, and assaults against innocent women and children, and they hold in contempt the daring bravery of men who sacrificed their lives for a country that continues to deny their dignity and humanity. Still, these courageous warriors dare to save their children and honor their grandparents. We know for certain that hope may be denied, and dreams deferred, but the souls of Black folk who defy such chicanery will rise, and our victory over death shall prevail.

This is my personal testimony, and I invite you to walk with me on the street where I lived. Watch how our promised land became purgatory. Hollywatts was deemed ground zero for the so-called "War on Drugs," as proclaimed by Ronald Wilson Reagan. Watch as the former Commander-in-Chief—implicated in the orchestration of the "Dark Alliance" with drug cartels who directly delivered death—helped to transform my community of Hollywatts from our promised land into purgatory.

I am a witness.

DECISIONS

The way Things Were
Isn't the Way They Are
Life's Ever Changing
Real Different by Far
Reflections on Youth
Reveal New Truth
About Decisions Once Made
Now Kept Up to Date
Goodness and Kindness
For the Rest of My Life
A Commitment Forever
To Treat Others Right
Decision to Be the Best I Can
No Turning Back
I Am the Man
Facing Tomorrow
Without A Doubt
God Gives the Victory
And Now I Can Shout

Two

We did not need a clock to tell the time of day. Every morning at 4:30, my father got out of bed to prepare for work. My mother followed him and arose at five o'clock.

Arthur Lawrence Cribbs and Hattie Dellena Morrison met in Memphis, Tennessee, during a horrific flood. Working with a recovery team, Arthur went door to door checking on the welfare of residents in the flood zone. One day, he walked up the steps to a white frame house on his route and knocked on the door. Hattie cracked the door open and saw a young, black man standing outside.

"Are you and your family alright?" Arthur inquired.

"Yes, thank you," Hattie replied. "My parents are attending to our store over on Chelsea Street, but we're fine here."

"I see you have a lot of good furniture in this room behind you," Arthur continued. "If the rain keeps falling, the flooding could hit your street and overflow into your home."

"What can we do?" Hattie asked.

"My men and I can help to move the furniture upstairs," he offered.

"Really? That would be great," Hattie said.

With that, Arthur instructed his team to join him in moving furniture from the living and dining rooms up to the second floor of the house. He and his men visited homes all around Memphis, but it quickly became obvious his interest in this house extended beyond its furnishings. Hattie had attracted his attention as well as his concern.

Moving the furniture upstairs was completed a lot faster than Arthur desired. Looking around the house, he realized there was nothing else to do. There was no reason for him to linger.

"I'll come back again later, maybe tomorrow, just to make sure everything is alright here," he told Hattie.

"Thank you for checking on us and moving all that heavy furniture. I'm sure my parents will greatly appreciate your courtesy," she told him.

"Well, I just want to make sure you are okay," he reiterated. "I'll see you tomorrow."

As Hattie closed the front door, Arthur backed away slowly and moved toward the truck with the two men who helped him move the heavy furniture.

"Arthur, you seemed to have taken a little extra time back there," chided Mac, the heavy-set teammate.

"That was one fine woman," Arthur said with a big grin on his face.

"Oh, you noticed that? I thought you were just making sure she and her family were safe from the flood," Mac continued. "Seems like now you have more than water on your mind."

Albert, the third member of the team, sat in the middle of the truck's front seat between Arthur, the driver, and Mac. The three men laughed in harmony and nodded in agreement.

True to his word, Arthur returned to Hattie's house shortly before noon the next morning.

Hattie opened the door wide and again thanked Arthur for helping her family.

"We're still fine," she told him. "Thanks for stopping by."

"That's great," Arthur said in a shy voice, as he looked down at his shoes and then glanced up again. "Once the weather clears and the water recedes, you might need some help getting all that furniture downstairs and back where it belongs," he suggested.

"I think we can handle it," Hattie replied with a tone that indicated she was independent and did not require any further assistance.

"Well, would you mind if I just came by sometime again and see how you are doing?" Arthur asked.

"Sure, if you'd like," Hattie said. "Thanks for dropping by this morning."

As the door closed slowly, Arthur lifted his heels, spun around, and tap-danced down the stairs to the sidewalk. His step was much lighter as he thought about the open-ended invitation to call on Hattie again. He decided to write her a note and ask her out on a date. He still had more work to do in the area, as the flooding had stopped but people needed help. The only real thing that mattered now was getting Hattie to go out with him.

A week passed before he was able to return to her home. He, Mac, and Albert finished their rounds and stopped for beers at Maxine's Bar and Grill. Arthur was anxious to see Hattie but did not want to give away his feelings to his buddies. He did tell his best friend, Owie Whitney, about the beautiful woman he had met during the flood. Arthur and Owie traded secrets all the time and never thought to keep vital information away from each other. Owie was happy about Arthur's find and knew Arthur planned to take Hattie to dinner that evening.

Upon arriving at Hattie's home, Arthur took a final look in the mirror to make sure his tie was knotted correctly and his hat cocked just right. He felt ready to present his best self to the young woman who welcomed him into her home during the flood.

As Hattie opened the door, she sniffed the odor of beer on his breath. Although he had brushed his teeth, the residue of alcohol was still there. "Have you been drinking?" she demanded.

"Oh, the guys and I just had a couple of beers after work," he told her. "I'm not drunk or anything."

"You've been drinking, and now you're at my door," her stern voice turned unfriendly. "Don't come around my house with alcohol on your breath."

Arthur felt the pain of rejection as Hattie offered no compromise or sympathy. Her determined look and serious words were more than instructive. They were final. Now, Arthur had to think quickly and make amends to the best of his ability.

"You're right, I'm sorry. That won't happen again—I promise," he assured. "But I'd still like to have dinner with you. How about tomorrow?" he asked.

"What? Tomorrow? We'll see." Hattie said with a slant hint of certainty.

Arthur smiled at her, and she returned his smile with laughter. "I'll see you tomorrow," he said with a lighter tone of voice that sounded more like singing than speaking. That was the beginning of an eighteen-month courtship that ended in marriage on June 28, 1938.

The newlyweds found an apartment in South Memphis. Hattie worked as a secretary in a downtown office. Arthur continued to drive trucks and make deliveries. Hattie was a devout Christian who attended Greater Mt. Zion Missionary Baptist Church. Arthur wasn't much of a churchgoer when they met, but he began to visit Hattie's church during their dating. After they were married, he became a regular member of her church, started going to Sunday school, and even returned for the Sunday night services.

He identified himself as a "race man" who followed the teachings of Marcus Garvey and was enthralled by the historian Carter G. Woodson. He began to read the Bible seriously as well. Although he had been on his own since he was twelve years old, he managed to learn how to read, write, and do arithmetic. His mother, Carrie James, was twenty years old and single when she gave birth. She died two days later because of medical complications.

His father, Daniel Cribbs, had been a neighbor to Carrie's family and lived only a couple of houses away. Daniel was twelve years her senior and married to another woman. He and his wife moved to St. Louis shortly after Arthur was born, leaving him to be raised by Carrie's sister, Meadie James.

Three years after Arthur and Hattie got married, World War II broke out. Steeped in Garvey's doctrine and fascinated by the leadership of Haile Selassie, emperor of Ethiopia, Arthur attempted to join the United States Army in 1941 with an ambition to become a part of the tank corps. His greatest desire was to go to Ethiopia and fight with the resistance against Italy. His hopes were dashed when the Army rejected him. Less than a year later, he was drafted by the United States Navy and became a member of its Construction Battalion (CBs). He was assigned to drive trucks, and his unit was eventually shipped overseas to the Philippines.

Driving trucks was very familiar to Arthur, but his greatest joy came with working on the engines and under the hoods of military vehicles. He was a mechanic to the core of his soul. Grease on his hands and a set of tools were all he needed to inspire his enthusiasm.

Working with the CBs was his ticket to doing what he loved. But his tour in the Philippines was abruptly interrupted when a crane dropped and landed on his back. Arthur was hospitalized for weeks in critical condition.

Doctors worked fiercely to save his life. After exhausting every medical procedure, they knew to keep him alive, they gave up. Years later, my father would tell me it was the Filipina nurses and his white navy chaplain, the Rev. Joseph Howard, who never surrendered nor gave up on his survival. Under the nurses' persistent care and the fervent prayers of Chaplain Howard, Arthur survived the crane accident. The Filipina nurses and his chaplain never left him alone and they were the only ones who stayed with him while he was in the hospital.

Chaplain Howard and my father became best friends. Their friendship lasted over many years—even through their separation in different states. After the war, Chaplain Howard went home to Texas where he became an instructor at Bishop College, an historically Black college run by the National Baptist Church, a predominately Black denomination.

In December 1945, my father returned to the United States and disembarked in Long Beach, California. He felt the warmth of the winter sun and saw tall, swaying palm trees along the streets of Los Angeles. He found a telephone booth and called his wife.

"Hattie," he started, "if we're going to stay married, we're going to live in Los Angeles."

Happy to hear her husband's voice but bewildered by his certainty, Hattie had some reluctance about leaving everything and everyone she knew so well. Only her love and devotion to Arthur gave her sufficient courage and the ability to give up one life and embrace another.

"Los Angeles?" she questioned over the long-distance telephone wires. "You want to live in Los Angeles?" It was more than a question. The idea of moving was not very intimidating; she and Arthur had done that when they left Memphis and stayed briefly in Chicago. They lived in the Windy City for a couple of years before he was sent to war. After Arthur was drafted into the Navy, they returned to Memphis so Hattie could be close to her parents.

"Yes! It's beautiful out here," he said, convincing himself as much as Hattie. "We can make a real life in California. I have a cousin who will take us in and help us out."

It took a little more than a month before Hattie made up her mind, packed her belongings, and caught a train to the West Coast. Along the way, her heart and mind were in conflict. Los Angeles is much farther away from Memphis than Chicago, and the three-day train trip in a seat with a carload of strangers did not appeal to her. Although she had friends who were also talking about going to California, she did not know anyone who was already there.

"My cousin Annette will be waiting for you," Arthur had assured Hattie. Annette Walker was the only person Arthur knew who had actually settled in Los Angeles and owned a home. She had never married but found her way around the city easily. The roads were laid out on a grid with avenues running north and south and many of the streets and boulevards going east and west. Annette had successfully established a small business. She owned her home and lived alone.

Hattie arrived on a Thursday afternoon, and Annette waited at Union Station to meet her train. Although she did not have a car and could not drive, Annette had ordered a car and driver to take her downtown and to return her with her cousin's wife back to her home in South Central Los Angeles.

Both women were meeting each other for the first time. Hattie had given Annette a description of herself and the clothes she would be wearing when the train pulled into Union Station. Annette had done the same with complete details of her clothing and her physical appearance. Annette saw Hattie first. Carrying an overnight case and a folded suit bag, Hattie stepped off the train wearing her favorite beige hat, beige purse, and matching beige shoes. She donned a vanilla crème colored dress and white gloves, which Annette thought was appropriate attire. She extended her hand and then wrapped her arms around Hattie's waist.

"You must be Hattie," Annette said while motioning to the driver to take the bag and case.

"And you must be Annette," Hattie responded. "Thank you for coming here to meet me. And thank you for allowing us to stay in your home," she added graciously.

"I'm so glad you're here," Annette replied. "Arthur can't stop talking about you. He wanted to be here, but the Navy wouldn't let him leave the base. He hopes to come to my house this weekend. He can't wait to see you."

"Go around to the parking lot near the baggage claim area so we can pick up Hattie's luggage," Annette instructed the driver.

The two women and the driver made their way through Union Station in Downtown Los Angeles. A crowd of people jammed the tunnel and hallway to the waiting area of the train station as Annette and her driver sought to collect Hattie's luggage. She had packed four large suitcases with winter clothes and boots.

"Child," Annette said, "You're in Southern California now. You're not going to need all those winter clothes here."

It was 67 degrees when Hattie stepped off the train in late January 1946. Not only had she left the snow and cold behind her, but her heart, soul, and mind remained in Memphis with her mother and stepfather. Her body had departed in search of her beloved husband and sought answers as to why Arthur had said that in order for their marriage to last, it could only happen in Los Angeles.

For Hattie, Los Angeles was a foreign land. She knew about Hollywood and its cinematic interpretation of life through the perspective of the movie industry. She never felt positive about the portrayal of people on the big screen in movie theaters. Now, upon her arrival, she was seeing the reality of Los Angeles and the bustle of postwar America. Chicago had barely prepared her for the pace and crowd in the emerging city. Chicago was older and established. Los Angeles was in its infancy, full of new buildings and freshly developed neighborhoods.

Upon her arrival on the West Coast, Hattie certainly was not at home. It was warm in January. People moved swiftly in the train terminal and even faster on the streets. Drivers drove swiftly through intersections and stop signs and traffic signals were treated more like suggestions rather than regulators of vehicles moving through the streets. Her new home in Los Angeles was off to a bustling start, and she had yet to see her beloved Arthur. Her mother, stepfather, and the people who made up her network of family and friends remained in Memphis. She only had one name in Los Angeles, and it was Arthur's cousin, Annette.

The knock at the front door occurred at 7:30 that Friday night, one day after Hattie had arrived at Annette's home. She found the house immaculate, with every item properly arranged. When she heard someone knocking at the door, Annette moved from her seat to open it. Standing there in his official navy-blue uniform, Arthur hugged his cousin, peeked his head inside the home, and spied his wife standing across the room.

Hattie and Arthur locked eyes on each other as their faces broadened and they raced toward each other. Both had their hands spread out wide as their bodies made contact and their lips locked. Annette suddenly became a spectator of the two lovers who seemed to have held each other much longer than she considered proper.

Tears crawled slowly down Arthur's and Hattie's cheeks. There was a mixture of hearty laughter, joyful weeping, and an unfamiliar strangeness between them. Annette was a witness.

"You are really here?" Arthur murmured with all the strength he could muster just above a whisper.

"Yes, I'm here. I made it," Hattie said through her crying laughter.

"Welcome to L.A., baby," Arthur smiled at Hattie. "How is everything back home? How are your parents?"

"I think they're okay," she said. "They're still running the business and making ends meet."

It had been nearly three years since the former newlyweds had seen each other. Through the course of the war, they had written to each other and sent a variety of messages through various sources. Hattie knew Arthur had been injured but was not sure to what extent. She wanted to know if he was still in pain. Did he get good treatment? Her rapid-fire questions rushed out of her mouth and intermingled with her glowing excitement. She was happy to have her husband back in her arms.

AFTER THE FIRE

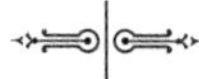

Burning without consuming
Flaming from afar
Caught Brother Moses' attention
He ran without a car
Running from himself
In Median he landed
Heard the Voice of God
And a staff he was handed
Charged to be a leader
People suffering without relief
Who am I to go home
He raised the question in disbelief
Called into service
There was no turning back
Pressed onward into struggle
God put Moses right on track

THREE

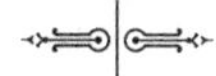

Like several families on the street where I lived, my grandparents left Memphis and followed their daughter and son-in-law to California in search of a warmer climate and kinder environment. Menard and Bessie Gordon shut down their business and headed west. They were a close-knit family, and the distance between Los Angeles and Memphis was far greater than their separation in Chicago. My grandmother never adjusted to her daughter, my mother, being away from her. Now, with a new granddaughter and another baby on the way, Bessie needed to be close to her only child, Hattie, who was now fully grown, married and independent.

"I know you are an adult and can get along just fine, but I want to see my grandbaby," Bessie convinced her only child.

My parents, Arthur and Hattie, had already established themselves in their new home in a residential housing development called George Washington Carver Manor.

With help from the GI Bill and both of their incomes, they were able to put the down payment on a new house. They found they could afford the monthly house note. Having her mother and stepfather around eased some of the strain Hattie faced raising her two babies. Menard was the only father Hattie had known. Bessie's first husband (who was my mother's actual father, Pervis Mosson) had divorced shortly after Hattie was born in Pine Bluff, Arkansas.

Throughout her life, Hattie thought her last name was Morrison, and it was the only name she used for herself. Many years later, while visiting her relatives in Memphis, Hattie learned her real name was Mosson and not Morrison. She never saw her real father after the divorce. But as a fully grown adult at that point in her life, Hattie did not care about the details of her real name. Menard Gordon was the only "father" she ever knew, and she loved him as her daddy.

"It doesn't really matter to me," Hattie told her cousin Sarah, who felt compelled to try and correct her about her real family name. "I've been Morrison all my life," Hattie concluded. "There's no need to change my name now."

Pervis Mosson and Bessie Bowen moved from Prentiss, Mississippi, where they met, to Pine Bluff, Arkansas. Although both had been young and adventurous when they left their homes in search of a larger world with more opportunities, their romance faded. Pervis had roving eyes and an appetite to satisfy his romantic urges away from Bessie. Their love evaporated and transformed into a deadly contest of wills and anger.

During a heated exchange after Bessie caught Pervis with another woman, their verbal assaults turned physically violent, and Pervis used his masculine strength against Bessie's more delicate defenses. Their battle resulted in Bessie suffering lacerations on her face and a deep gut punch to her very pregnant stomach. She ended up in the hospital emergency room and barely survived the brutal battle. Her unborn baby was not so fortunate and was killed in her womb.

Bessie recovered, picked up her life, and moved to Memphis to escape a husband who had exhibited violence against her in their Arkansas home. It was an easy move for her, since her sister Etta Mae lived in Memphis and offered her a room to stay. Etta was married to Roy Robinson and had a home with space for Bessie and her toddler, Hattie. "There is always room for family," Etta assured her older sister.

It didn't take long for Bessie to establish herself in Memphis by doing domestic work in the homes of white families. She was determined to become independent, find her own path, and follow her nature. Shortly after arriving in Memphis, she met her life partner. Bessie and Menard Gordon got married and opened their own business.

Known for her cooking and baking skills, she opened a café. The featured items on the menu were Bessie's homemade butter rolls, fried chicken, collard greens, potato salad, and peach cobbler. Her sweetened iced tea and hot coffee also brought customers in the door. Eventually, Bessie and Menard were able to buy a house and create a place for Hattie to play and grow up.

Hattie was a highly intelligent little girl who discovered her independence very early in life. She also developed advanced athletic skills and could handle a basketball as well as any kid in her high school. Hattie joined the Memphis Chicks, a women's basketball team, and played point guard. She was the classic triple threat: smart, athletic, and attractive.

One day, while reminiscing about the different twists her life had taken, Hattie thought about suitors who passed through her young adulthood but didn't have the qualities she expected in a mate. After she met Arthur, her heart followed the passion that possessed her total being. She could not take him off her mind. Shortly after they married, she moved with him from her parents' home in Memphis to Chicago. It was a relatively brief stay in the Windy City before they moved back to Memphis, where Arthur was drafted into the United States Navy as World War II escalated. It was part of the unforeseen journey that eventually resulted in them settling in California.

When Hattie's long-distance call came through, her mother wanted to be assured that her only daughter had made it safely to Los Angeles, and that she was comfortable and able to survive on her own so far away.

"Mother, I'm your daughter," Hattie reminded my grandmother. "You raised me to take care of myself and not depend on anybody."

"I know, baby," Bessie consoled herself. "But you're at the Pacific Ocean, and Lord only knows how big and faraway that is."

"I'm fine, Momma. How are you and Poppa doing?" she inquired to divert the conversation. "How's the café?"

"We're good. Business is great. Everybody asks about you," Bessie confided. "Now, whenever you want to come back home, you always have a place to stay."

"Thank you, Momma. Arthur's cousin, Annette, is really sweet and kind and she has taken me in," Hattie assured her mother. "Arthur and I are doing just fine. He should be leaving the Navy soon."

"I'm so glad Artie is okay," Bessie said. "Was he hurt very badly over there in those Philippines?"

"He got seriously injured," Hattie responded. "He almost got killed but, God have mercy, he's back, and he looks really good."

"Sweetie, I know you have gone head over heels about that man," Bessie chuckled.

"He is my husband. I love him so much, and he loves me," Hattie giggled. "And you know his name is Arthur and not Artie. He doesn't like you calling him that."

"Well, he's Artie to me," Bessie smirked. "I know he's a nice man and helped to rescue us during the big flood. You know I like him."

"I know. Well, look, Arthur will be coming home soon," Hattie began to conclude the long-distance phone call. "I love you, Momma."

"I love you, too, baby. Bye now," Bessie said as she hung up the phone.

After that call, it was about three years before Bessie and Menard closed their café and took the train west to Los Angeles. The early spring weather felt more like summer than the end of winter. Union Station was larger than the train station in Memphis and fancier than any building Bessie had ever seen in person. There were people who filled the waiting room dressed in fancy city clothes. There were more cars, buses, and street cars than she had ever seen at one time all moving rapidly in various directions. The scene outside the train station made Bessie slightly dizzy.

Hattie and Arthur were standing on the platform when the train's engine pulled into the station. Bessie was dressed in her fox stole, matching navy-blue purse and shoes, and a wide brim navy-blue hat. She had seen the hat in a magazine and decided she could make one by hand. She wore a navy-blue dress that accented her figure, with a navy-blue belt around her waist.

"Welcome to Los Angeles," her son-in-law greeted her. "Hello, Mr. Gordon," Arthur reached out to shake his father-in-law's hand. The two men smiled and grabbed hands.

"I am so glad you are safely back from the war." Menard welcomed Arthur like he was the one returning home and had just arrived back home off the train.

The genuine respect between the elder Gordon and the young warrior was evident to the other passengers and their awaiting families.

"Let's get your luggage and get out of here," Arthur offered. "We are in the parking lot just outside the baggage area."

The distance and difference between Memphis and Los Angeles were far greater than the 1,800 miles that separated them. In addition to the early spring weather, which was normally chilly in Memphis but in Los Angeles burned Bessie's skin, people in Southern California walked faster and talked with the rapid fire of a machine gun. They dressed more casually in public than the folk back home, and they lacked manners, courtesy, or politeness, as Bessie observed. Everybody seemed to be in a hurry no matter where they were going or what they were doing. Bessie thought about what she was witnessing and how she was feeling about the sudden impression of her new hometown.

Hattie had prepared her mother and stepfather with the good news about her new neighbors who were also from Memphis.

"Can you believe it, we are surrounded by people who moved to California from both North and South Memphis," Hattie said with pride.

She wanted to help ease some of her mother's anxiety about living in a foreign place. Now, Menard and Bessie were about to become Californians. Bessie was observing people in that New South. To her, many of them seemed to have lost their minds.

When Arthur drove his 1948 Plymouth into the driveway of his new home, a small group of people were standing outside ready to greet them. Willie and Fannie Thomas were holding a pan of barbecue and two sweet potato pies. Dorothy and James Gadberry waved as the family exited the vehicle and she was holding a potato salad. Camille and Herman Murphy were there with a covered pan of home baked dinner rolls and a case of soda pop.

"We're the Carver Manor Memphis Club," welcomed Herman with a grin that stretched across his face. "Welcome to L.A.!" the small group shouted in chorus.

Bessie and Menard melted in the warm reception of gratitude, as they were the special guests of honor in their daughter's new neighborhood. A flurry of questions flew toward them as they made their way along the sidewalk and into the house. The voices were jumbled together as everyone wanted to know the news from Memphis. Suddenly, the divide between the Ole South and South Central Los Angeles was not too great. In fact, the gulf had been bridged by Southern hospitality and delicious homemade cooking.

Right behind the welcoming party, Marcus and Mildred Clackman arrived from a couple of houses away. U.S. Army Lieutenant Robert Page and his wife, Maxine, made the short walk from their house situated right next door to Arthur's and Hattie's home. Walking from directly across the street came Bob and Bernice Kirkland. Also strolling into the house were Daddy and Mother Wofford, as everyone referred to them, making the walk from around the corner, where their property abutted Hattie and Arthur's new home. Another elderly couple known only as Mother and Daddy Smith stepped quickly from their home next to the Thomas house across the street. Also making his way from around the corner was Mack Johnson, who arrived with a couple of large watermelons and long stalks of sweet corn.

The Gadberrys lived next door to the Clackman's home and made their way to greet the new arrivals from their hometown of Memphis. Dorothy Gadberry had slipped away from her mother and family to board the train on her way to the "City of Angels." Her war veteran husband called her from California with news he had no intention of returning to Tennessee. Like my father, Mr. Gadberry told his wife if they were going to remain married, it would only happen on the West Coast in Southern California. He had seen too much on the battlefield and remembered too much from growing up in the defenseless, hate-filled American South to go back there and settle on those unsettling grounds.

Fannie and Willie Thomas lived across the street from Hattie and Arthur. Eventually, they would become my godparents. They were urban missionaries who trekked around our neighborhood and drove across town to assist families who called for help. The fortunate recipients of their merciful house calls and visits were often treated to one of Mother Thomas' homemade cakes or pies. Baking and cooking were her trademark and talent. Collard greens, black-eyed peas, cornbread, and mashed potatoes often accompanied them as they traveled across town or across the street to call on the sick and shut-in individuals and the families they visited.

Often, their succulent meals provided the side dishes to Daddy Thomas' barbecued chicken and ribs (beef and pork). Like my family, they may have left Memphis in their rearview mirror, but Daddy and Mother Thomas brought the best of Tennessee with them to California. And they were not alone.

"Hi, neighbor" was shouted by Mr. Clackman from a house two doors away once the unfamiliar face became familiar and the ties to a family or neighbor were known. A friend or relative of one neighbor became a friend to others on our street. That short, simple phrase was an intentional reminder of a relationship that had meaning and prompted support for each other.

In those early days of dreaming and building a safe haven, common stories and experiences that had driven families to leave their native Southern places of birth painted a picture of hope and opportunity out west in Southern California. The patterns and rhythms of their pasts in the old South were transported through them to the new South and its radiant sunshine and nearby beaches.

Each family had a different story but very similar reasons for moving to California. Now, they found themselves together on the same street living merely a few houses apart, despite being unaware of each other prior to moving into the newly constructed homes in Carver Manor—a neighborhood some people called the "promised land." Blacks who arrived in the warm, sunlit streets of Los Angeles, regardless of their valor and patriotism on the battlefields during the war, remained unwanted anywhere outside the specified blocks in this South Central Los Angeles corridor. In order to maintain racial decorum throughout Greater Los Angeles, our homes were built to give Blacks a place to live without becoming enticed to move into areas reserved for "whites only."

Doctors, accountants, educators, lawyers, beauticians, and other professionals resided next door to custodians, postal workers, railroad porters, and winos. They were there together. And as far as my father was concerned, everybody on our street was his neighbor.

SWEET BYE 'N' BYE

Grandma standing
at the window
Over her kitchen sink
Saying, "Hello," to each one passing by
While humming
an old Dr. Watts
Gently under her breath
"I love the Lord,
He heard my cry"
Singing, remembering,
and praying
Away her pain
While giving praise
to God and
Sharing her joy
for living
Not in vain
"Oh, Lord, here I am
Knee-bent"

Many years
had come and gone
Moving from the South
to West
Too many friends
had passed on to a better place than this
"This little light of mine
I'm gonna let it shine"
In the darkness of the night
When the birds are fast asleep
I can hear my grandmother singing
Praying to God to keep us safe

FOUR

Arthur was still in the military and lived on the Navy base. His service time was coming to an end as the war was officially over, and his time was running out. The important thing for him now was to get a job, find a home or place to stay, and learn his way around Los Angeles. He had already started talking to his war buddies and was planning to separate from the Navy. He quickly discovered there were plenty of other Black servicemen who also decided to stay in Los Angeles. They all were in the same predicament. The sprawling metropolis was on the verge of a population explosion.

Arthur was certain he did not want to return to the South. He had no plans to go back to Memphis and the racial division that defined his life there, nor did he have the desire to weather another cold winter in Chicago. The bright sunshine and warm January wind were more than sufficient to convince him he had found his dreamland.

While on the ship coming back to the States from the Philippines, Arthur had already begun making plans for his future and his family. He would enroll in technical college to become a certified automotive and diesel engines mechanic. He would find a job to support Hattie and himself. They would find a neighborhood where they could afford to buy a house and raise children. For her part, Hattie would start looking for work and help Annette with anything she needed. Arthur thought the GI Bill was a good source to get him started. He had heard about it and figured if the United States government would help pay for his education and purchase a home, he was on his way.

A war veteran who nearly made the ultimate sacrifice for his country in a foreign land should not have any worries about getting government support. Like many of his fellow Black warriors, World War II was not just a victory over Germany and Japan, it was a Double V victory to end discrimination and open new doors for America's courageous, loyal, and good citizens who were Black. He served his country with pride and dignity. His country would now return the favor by honoring his humanity. Arthur believed winning the war overseas would induce the United States to defeat racial bigotry and hatred at home. He thought starting his life over in Los Angeles, in liberal California, was the first step toward a better, brighter future.

Hattie found work very quickly after she answered an ad from the McDonnell-Douglass Aircraft Company looking for workers who could help to build a fleet of new airplanes. What attracted her attention was the location of the aircraft plant in Long Beach. She figured that would bring her and Arthur closer together. She thought working near the naval base would give them more time to see each other, and she could make money to help buy a house. Now, she had a plan and was more than ready to put it into operation.

Fighting wars for America did not move the nation very far from its racial divisions and well-honed bigotry. Although Arthur and Hattie had moved away from Memphis, Tennessee, in the segregated South, they found themselves in a more sophisticated but still extremely racist Southern California. The warm days attracted a blend of Southerners who transported their cultures, attitudes, and traditions across the country.

Hatred toward Black folk now expanded to include Mexicans and Native Americans who were eternally long-term residents in this New South. Jews and Catholics did not fare much better, as the White Anglo-Saxon Protestants established new neighborhoods and structured certain protocols to create and retain pure communities of their own kind. They structured their own communities with reenforced social norms that were protected by law enforcement agencies. To meet the growing demands of an expanding metropolis, law enforcement agencies hired men who were Southern-born transplants to Southern California.

In the words of the Saturday night television host Tennessee Ernie Ford, "Hold on to those Confederate Dollars, folks, because the South will rise again." Indeed, Arthur, Hattie, and their neighbors quickly discovered that life as they knew it back home was working its way to Hollywatts.

It was like an undetectable virus brewing barely below the surface, inching its way into the lives of young boys and girls. It was too evil to imagine or perceive such human treachery was conceived in our promised land. The hopes and dreams our parents prided themselves in crafting for their children were no match for the deliberate schemes designed to alter the course of their innocent lives.

In August 1965, news reports blared across the country about the human explosion dubbed the "Watts Riots." The conflict broke out in South Los Angeles after a motorist, Marquette Frye, was stopped by a California Highway Patrolman on Avalon Avenue about a mile west of my home. Tension was already high in our area because people felt they had not been seen, heard, or considered worthy of protection from police harassment. Being stopped by cops and brutalized was not rare or unexpected.

I once found myself forced to lie flat, faced down on the ground by members of the Los Angeles County Sheriff's Department while just around the corner from my home. I was walking home from the Boys Club after practicing for the Junior Olympics. If there was a consolation for such an encounter, I did win a gold medal in the 440-yard relay as the first leg on our track team. Such stop-and-frisk procedures were routine for many Black men and young boys in Hollywatts. That was my first such encounter. It would not be my last.

Shortly after the riots began, Cal-Trans (California Department of Transportation) held a public hearing just west of Watts at a hotel near the Los Angeles International Airport. That event was nothing short of a sham, a vile exhibition of "standard operating procedures" when it came to well-honed practices of treating people in Hollywatts as insignificant objects. The hearing was held to take testimony from residents whose neighborhoods would be directly affected by a planned new freeway that would run from the east side of Los Angeles County in the City of Norwalk to the west side near the city of El Segundo at the Pacific Ocean. Our community, Hollywatts, was situated right in the path of the proposed construction. The irony—the insult—of the public hearing was not lost on anyone.

The room inside the International Airport Hotel was packed with people from across Los Angeles County.

From Beverly Hills to Watts, people showed up and spoke up to protest their opposition and to fight to protect their communities from the potential harm the freeway would impose.

While state highway officials were conducting their hearing, Watts was literally blowing up. The explosions erupted throughout South Central Los Angeles like a wave of violence bombarding the core of the "City of Angels," as Los Angeles was dubbed. The riots continued for six days and were a direct result of years of frustration and police brutality without relief or resolve.

Our delegation from Watts, Willowbrook, and Hollywatts stood in opposition to the construction proposal that would divide, destroy, and wall off parts of our community. Another delegation from Beverly Hills similarly expressed their opposition to such a development going through their upscale city, seeing the benefits as negligible. They saw what we saw: if the freeway was constructed and ran through our neighborhoods, it would interfere with the aspirations of families concerned about the health and safety of their children.

At the time of the hearing, my mother was employed at the California Department of Transportation. She was aware of the plans and was determined to voice her concerns. My mother and grandmother prepared their testimonies and drove several of our neighbors with them to the hearing to testify. They were the embodiment of a people rendered invisible and unheard. The exact same elements that ignited the Watts Riots were being played out publicly right in front of us under the auspices of the State of California.

My grandmother and mother stood at the podium and mustered the audacity to express their opposition to and their concerns about the proposed freeway. Such a development would divide our neighborhood, rearrange access to local streets, and transform the tenor and content of our community. Some of our neighbors would lose their homes and they would be forced to move and find somewhere else to live. Traffic overflow on the freeway would clog community passage and create disadvantages in our area that already suffered from being underserved. Unfortunately, being ignored by public officials was standard fare for many people in South Central Los Angeles.

Their testimonies and appeals were eloquent, accurate, passionate, and ineffective to save our community. What my mother already knew was that the plans to construct the freeway had been determined even before the hearing was called. At best, the public had been invited to speak up long after the state had decided to build the New Century Freeway a mere nine blocks north from the street where we lived. The painful irony of the charade of the public hearing was that it was held on Friday afternoon, a mere three days after the Watts Riots had erupted and the flames of burning buildings flared and smoke choked the entire City of Los Angeles. The echoing cry, "Burn, Baby, Burn," was still spreading across the Southland.

Yet one woman who did manage to develop a close, personal relationship with a public official was my grandmother. She would often pick up the telephone and call our county supervisor, Kenneth Hahn, with requests for service. He would personally take her calls and acted expeditiously and directly. He visited our home and would show up at our church upon her request or at her invitation.

"Mr. Hahn, this is Bessie Gordon," my grandmother would announce over the telephone line.

"Yes, Mrs. Gordon, I recognize your voice. How are you? How is your family?" he inquired.

"Everybody here is doing just fine, Mr. Hahn. Thank you for asking," was my grandmother's standard reply.

"How can I help you today?" Supervisor Hahn continued.

"We need a stop sign or a light signal on Compton Avenue to slow down some of this traffic," she would explain.

"Let me look into that and get back to you," the supervisor informed her.

"We would really appreciate that. Thank you for taking my call," she concluded.

"You know you can call me anytime," he said before hanging up the phone.

That's how my grandmother helped to get things done in our neighborhood. Unable to read or write, she used her voice on behalf of our community. She worked to bring the first swimming pool to the area and was part of the development of George Washington Carver Park. It was located right behind and next to our elementary school, also named after the Tuskegee scientist.

My grandmother called Supervisor Hahn and asked him to help find me a job. Her ties and direct, personal appeal were successful. I started working after school at the Willowbrook Public Library when I was in the eleventh grade. It was the first Los Angeles County public library.

My grandmother was unafraid and never intimidated by anyone, regardless of their station or status. People were just people to her. She listened carefully, observed intently, and spoke up whenever necessary. Community and public service defined Bessie Gordon. Her love for her family, her neighbors and her church drove her to act fearlessly and to use her voice to make improvements. Growing up in Mississippi under the harsh and cruel brutality of Southern bigotry, racism, and denied opportunities did not deter her. Instead, it formed within her a solid bedrock of tenacity and determination. She was a force to be reckoned with when necessary.

On the street where we lived, Bessie Gordon was not alone. There were others just like her, including fathers, grandfathers, mothers, grandmothers among our neighbors who forged a front against the tide of disappointment and institutionalized discrimination. Together, they formed a soulful, faithful fortress that was erected to protect and preserve their promises of a much better and brighter future for their families and children. What they missed, despite their vigilance, were the unseen forces focused on undermining their dreams and goodwill.

I DIDN'T KNOW

I didn't know
We were po'
And lived in a ghetto
It was home
Where kids could roam
And never felt left all alone
We were family
Living in community
Our strength was our unity
Unpretentious
Loving justice
Being just us

FIVE

Dr. George Semore, a graduate of Meharry Medical College in Nashville, Tennessee, lived around the corner from our house. He was our family doctor. In fact, he was the doctor for almost every family on our street and in the neighborhood. His middle-of-the-night medical house calls kept him busy after office hours. Dr. Semore delivered both my sisters and me into the world. His general medical practice covered whatever ailed his patients. We were very fortunate to have him as a neighbor. The closest hospital to our street was twelve miles away, and we had to negotiate congested city streets to get there in an emergency.

One night, my father and mother were away when I had my most severe asthma attack. My grandmother was home with my sisters and me. Bessie Gordon had her own remedies for childhood sickness, but that night she exhausted all her cures without abating the shortness of breath that choked my lungs. The fright in her eyes and her tired voice forecast her frustration and fear. Her only grandson was critically ill, and she didn't know what to do. Dr. Semore was with another patient and not available to make an immediate stop at our home. My grandmother began to pray. Then, like a bolt of lightning she jumped up and raced to the telephone.

There was another call she could make. With unsteady fingers, she began dialing a phone number that was familiar to her from a program she listened to on the radio. She managed to remember the number perfectly. Soon, I felt her hands pressing the telephone headset to my ear as I laid in bed barely taking in air. On the other end of the line, I heard the voice of a woman. Although I could not make out what she was saying, it was clear she was praying for me to get well.

Everything in the room turned grey. There was no color anywhere. My grandmother started crying while standing over me. Tears streamed down her chestnut-colored face. She held my hand and continued to press the phone hard against my tilted head. I listened. The woman's words became clearer and easier to understand, and the grayness of my world gave way to sepia then full color. The light in my room turned suddenly bright. I could see and hear. My breathing eased. My body felt light. My own voice echoed each word the lady on the phone said.

"Heal right now, Lord," I heard myself repeating. "Thank you for blessing me with good health," I continued.

Suddenly, I heard the rumbling sound of a car entering our driveway. No voices. One door opened and slammed. Then, the other door slammed shut behind it. My parents had finally arrived home. My grandmother rushed to our front door and opened it before my mother and daddy stepped inside our home.

"Junior is having an asthma attack," my grandmother shouted with her crackling voice.

Daddy entered my bedroom and saw the phone tucked under my ear. I continued to repeat each word as the woman on the other end of the line prayed. My father stood over me and watched, waited, and listened.

"Thank you," I mumbled to the praying lady on the other end of the phone line.

"I called the prayer line," I heard my grandmother explaining to my mother in the living room. "I didn't know what else to do. I was so scared," she confessed.

"I'll take him to the hospital," my father quickly declared. Daddy had made that trip many times with me. He wrapped me in a blanket, picked me up, and carried me to our car parked in the driveway. The crisp night air swept across my face as Daddy dug into his pockets to find his car key. Quickly, we were on our way to Harbor General Hospital in Torrance.

Daddy carried me in his arms as he raced into the emergency room. Fortunately, it was a quiet night. Doctors and nurses were available to see me upon arrival. I was sleepy but was breathing and feeling better. The asthma attack was over. The doctor pressed his stethoscope to my back and said, "Take a deep breath." The cold metal made me shiver but I inhaled and quickly pushed out warm air from my mouth. "Good," the doctor said. "Take another breath." I followed his commands as I sat up on the gurney.

"I don't hear any wheezing, and his lungs sound clear," the doctor said as he turned to the nurse. My father relaxed and a smile curled up on his face. That late-night bout was the last time I ever had an asthma attack. I have been a true believer in the power of prayer ever since that night, when a woman I did not know prayed for me over the telephone.

The impact of a stranger was a testament to the commitment of our community. Anonymous interactions were a rarity, and they were only temporary until faces and names became familiar. We lived in a true and functional neighborhood before that term was reduced to and rendered as "The Hood." Carver Manor was a safe place to walk, live, and attend school. I used to say, "I played in Watts and studied in Compton."

A vision of creating a future unlike their recent past energized our mothers and fathers, our grandparents, and their siblings to "make a way out of no way." The homes on our street were opened to children, relatives, friends, and new arrivals. Between paychecks, a knock on the door would bring a request for a cup of flour, to borrow an egg, get a can of beans, or to ask if anyone had time to watch over somebody's child until a parent or grandparent returned home from work.

My parents ensured our home was a welcoming space for anyone to enter. And for many years people literally came from around the world and stayed with us. Some were there only briefly, while others discovered a haven of warmth and Black Southern hospitality.

The Chin family, who came to the United States from China, was one of those families that discovered a new home in my parents' house. Dr. Chin studied pathology and worked in the lab at the new Martin Luther King Hospital that was built directly across the street from our home in Hollywatts. Mrs. Chin found a job as a domestic in a home about fifteen miles away in Long Beach. Their son, Sammy, commuted to work every day in Chinatown near downtown Los Angeles. Their daughter, Cindy, attended the same junior high school that my sisters and I had gone to near Hollywatts. Cindy was a straight-A student. Although she and her family had only arrived in the United States a mere three weeks before the school year began, Cindy was able to negotiate English and mastered the language quickly. Her ability to learn was astonishing and encouraging.

The Chins did not own a car, so Mrs. Chin spent every week at the home where she worked and only came back to our house on weekends to be with her husband and children. Her pattern of mobility was very familiar to our family.

Like Mrs. Chin, my grandmother did domestic work for Jewish families in Beverly Hills and Encino. She would leave our home early Monday morning or late Sunday night to go to work. We did not see her again until Friday, when my father or mother or both would drive to wherever my grandmother was working and bring her back home to Hollywatts.

Living in our home, the Chins became a part of our family. In fact, anyone who lived under our roof was family regardless of bloodline, nationality, race, or religion. Several Haitian men stayed in our home and referred to my mother as "Mother Cribbs," a designation of endearment. Because of my parents' openness, people from many different walks of life found their way to Hollywatts and experienced Black Southern hospitality around every corner and among our neighbors.

Every Christmas, Dr. Chin would take the bus to downtown Los Angeles and make his way through Chinatown to purchase his annual roasted duck and tea-soaked eggs. Those were his special treats and gifts to our family. Our home was a place of peace, prayer, and purpose.

Perhaps one of the most significant aspects of who our parents were and how they honored human life irrespective of a person's race, religion, gender, or social standing was their genuine compassion and open hospitality.

Arthur and Hattie Cribbs demonstrated their profound human capacity to receive everyone and accept them just as they were. No matter the person, the cause, the destination, or the distinction, my parents were available to respond to a call from anyone in need at any hour of the day or night.

One summer, my father's naval chaplain from Texas, the Rev. Joseph Howard, came and stayed with us. The afternoon Chaplain Howard showed up at our door, he became the first white man to enter and stay at our home over night. In fact, he remained with us for several days. His appearance was not so novel since we had seen many white people on television. Only Nat King Cole and the few Black characters on *Amos 'n' Andy* broke the stream of visual whiteness that entertained us on TV. Chaplain Howard had a gentle manner in speech and presence. What made him stand out, however, was his heavy Southern drawl.

Although almost everyone in our neighborhood had migrated from the South, the tone emanating from Chaplain Howard's throat was particularly distinct and very Southern. Yet, there was much more to the man than his whiteness and Southern accent. He was a Texan, a gentleman, and a God-fearing preacher who personified his sermons.

Chaplain Joe Howard was recognized among Black clergy and church leaders across the country. The Rev. Dr. J. Alfred Smith, Sr., pastor of Allen Temple Baptist Church in Oakland, California, counted Chaplain Howard among his dearest and closest friends.

Chaplain Howard's commitment to my injured father in the Philippines bonded those warrior-veterans through the duration of the war, and they retained their friendship in peacetimes. Chaplain Howard's placement at Bishop College during the extended period of segregation put him among a noble cadre of white professionals who practiced their skills at Historically Black Colleges and Universities across the Southern United States.

When Chaplain Howard arrived at our home, he entered a neighborhood of newly found friends. That was the way people treated each other in Hollywatts, as friends and neighbors, because many of them were World War II veterans. Anyone who arrived on our street as a stranger was swiftly welcomed and received as a new friend or neighbor to other people on our block.

I could still recall the sensation of returning home from elementary school and walking up and down the street on our block or going around the corner. I thought about my excitement when our family used to return from a long, cross-country trip. I began to remember how our neighborhood took on a completely different atmosphere on those Fridays back then.

Weekends were more than the approaching days of rest, recreation, and religion. The drums would beat out the strain of our parents and neighbors who were forced to comply with foreign rules and unyielding gestures in order to conform to values that were not their own. The drums brought forth comfort, continuity, and community.

On the street where I lived, the weekly rituals carried families from five days of labor and separation to two days of unity among neighbors, friends, and visiting cousins. Bicycles would compete with skates, as youngsters filled the sidewalks rolling around street corners at a rapid pace to avoid indoor chores before we were summoned to our homes for supper.

Every word, every greeting among our neighbors was an act of reinforcing a commitment to build a community. Just about every neighbor on the street where I lived depended on each other to keep a promise to build a safe place for children to play and families to thrive. There was no ambiguity about how much my daddy loved our neighborhood. He had an open and truly genuine affection based on conditions in the South that caused him and many other people to look out for each other.

"Hi, neighbor!" I would hear my daddy's familiar calling to Wilma's father, Mr. Willie Clackman. They lived just two houses away from us. My daddy had driven our 1948 four-door, grey-greenish Plymouth sedan into our driveway and parked. As he slipped out the driver's door, he waved to our neighbor. That was his daily ritual, and Mr. Clackman returned the salutation with the expected response, "Hey, neighbor."

Mr. Clackman and my daddy had served separately during World War II. Mr. Clackman had been in the army while my father was in the navy. The fact that they were now neighbors also meant they were survivors.

Mr. Clackman grew up in Oklahoma and wore the features of Native American Muskogee blood on his face. He was comparatively tall next to my father, who was barely five feet in height but who also shared the bloodlines of Native Americans who were Mississippi Choctaw. Every day, both men arrived home about the same time and exchanged their familiar greetings. We could set our clocks by our fathers' consistent patterns. It was always the same "Hi, neighbor" around five o'clock in the late afternoon.

Ours was an urban village where storytelling and drumming were sources of entertainment while neighbors, friends, and visitors congregated in garages and kitchens or on front lawns and in backyards. Those were the arenas to collect news and exchange the latest gossip. Doors remained unlocked during the day, and windows were raised and remained opened throughout the hot, steamy summer nights. But amid that tranquility lurked an unsuspecting demon. Transformation of our promised land quietly slithered up our streets and crawled around corners.

TWIN CHAMPIONS

Decide Now
To Do What We Can
Together We Struggle
Onward We Climb
Righteousness and Justice
Twin Champions of Faith
Lead Us and Guide Us
Persuade Us We Pray
Powerful and Free
Our Heads Held High
Nothing Can Stop Us
Not Even the Sky
Above the Strain
Beyond Our Gain
We Decide Our Fate
Whatever the Pain
Glory to God
All Praises We Sing
Each Breath We Take

Renews Us Again
Unafraid, Unashamed
The Way God Made Us
Chocolate, Purple
Darker Than Blue
One People Together
Build Community and Love
In the Spirit That Comes
From Heaven Above

Six

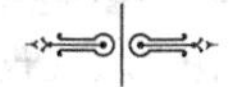

It is not lost on keen observers that while the Vietnam War was escalating and the number of our warrior sons and brothers were coming home in body bags, 1968 also was the year Dr. Martin Luther King, Jr. was assassinated while standing on the balcony of the Lorraine Motel in Memphis, Tennessee.

Just exactly one year earlier on April 4, 1967, he preached his most strident sermon against the war at the Riverside Church in New York City. He said, "We must rapidly begin the shift from a 'thing-oriented' society to a 'person-oriented' society. When machines and computers, profit motives, and property rights are considered more important than people, the giant triplets of racism, extreme materialism, and militarism are incapable of being conquered."

Unlike his most famous "I Have a Dream" speech given in 1963 at the March on Washington, Dr. King's sermon four years later put a death warrant on him. He expanded his vision and concerns beyond civil rights and took a deeper dive into the well of political, social, and economic justice and morality. By so doing, he assaulted the military apparatus of America. He had crossed the line into a spiritual and moral collaboration that put him in conflict with the expansive "military industrial complex". Someone somewhere in the upper echelon of government determined Dr. King crossed the line from civil rights to foreign policy. He ventured into the realm beyond domestic tranquility and into economic adventurism. It cost him his life. He paid the ultimate price.

Although the nation's leaders did not heed his wisdom and insight, they preferred his "Dream" speech and detested his prophetic voice in opposition to America's foreign policy and his passion for domestic peace. Perpetual war was only beginning to emerge as the unmentionable underpinning of America's immoral foreign policy.

The war in Vietnam became a corporate adventure into the extreme commercialism of perpetual war around the globe. On the street where I lived, sons, brothers, fathers, uncles, and cousins joined neighbors and friends in the buildup of the country's commitment to elevate the expansive development of an emerging military industry.

Dr. King's commitment to nonviolent protests throughout the South to advance social progress for Black people swerved in a more expansive direction. For all the times his life was put at risk, people in high places of power in America's political and corporate infrastructure determined he had gone too far and stepped outside the lines of racial justice. His sermon in New York put a larger target on his back, and his life was doomed without the ability to roll back his statements or persuade America's leaders to take a different course. A collision of differences resulted in the unaltering determination to eliminate the preacher and to perpetuate war in Vietnam.

The year 1968 was painfully horrific for many families in Hollywatts. The sons of World War II veterans were drafted and sent to Vietnam. In defiance of slain President John F. Kennedy's warning and resistance, but under the orders of his successor, the United States found itself embroiled in the merciless, protracted war in the jungles of that Southeast Asia nation. Like many young men in my neighborhood who were of draft age, I expected to be called up—although my perspective on war had changed radically after high school.

A Congressional appointee to the United States Naval Academy, my life shifted substantially only two days after graduating from Centennial High School in Compton, California. For five years since seventh grade, my only ambition and singular focus was on entering my plebe year in Annapolis, Maryland. The protracted process was laced with eliminations of ambitious young men, all high school students, who shared my objective to serve America with a commitment to the Navy. Receiving my appointment from Congressman Augustus Freeman Hawkins just three months before graduation was the hardest hurdle to overcome in the very competitive process. The final step in the process was to complete and pass a two-day medical physical at the U.S. Naval Hospital in Long Beach, California.

As a year-round athlete who competed in baseball, football, basketball, and track with a gold medal from the Junior Olympics on the Southern Area Boys Club's track team, my confidence soared upon receiving my Congressional appointment. It had been many years since that last asthma attack in the middle of the night. My health was good, and I felt the medical examination was pro forma and the final act before my admission to the Naval Academy.

As I watched the number of applicants decrease from about seventy in my area to only five, the persistent presence of my high school counselor, Miss Eliza Bryant, served to comfort me and increase my confidence. She walked that path with me every step of the way. By the time we reached near the end of the entrance process, eighteen months had passed, and that one last step stood between the Academy and me.

Vietnam seemed a long way away from Hollywatts. Some of my draft-aged neighbors had been called up. Jeff

Tyler, a neighbor whose mother babysat my sisters and me while our parents were at work, got drafted into the Army. Jeff was a quiet young man who was fascinated by motorcycles and automotive mechanics. He was playful, kind, and a good friend. Like me, Jeff was an only son with three sisters compared to my two. I never heard him raise his voice or engage in an argument. Suddenly, he was gone.

"I never hurt anybody in my life," Jeff began to explain at his father's funeral many years later and long after the Vietnam War was over. "They made me a killer," he continued. "I got drafted and ended up in Nam, and I had to kill people I didn't know. They never did anything to me except fight to protect themselves and their families. I was forced to kill them." The perpetual nightmare of going to war in a distant land never evaded Jeff's memory.

Jeff's father, Mr. Marcus Tyler, had fought in World War II. Like my dad, men in our neighborhood rarely talked about their war experiences and being overseas. Mr. Tyler had served in Europe as part of the Red Ball Express, a truck convoy comprised mostly of African American soldiers, which ran food supplies and other materials across battle lines. They drove almost 6,000 trucks immediately following the successful Normandy Invasion in 1944.

Like most of the Black men who returned home after the war, Mr. Tyler rarely talked about his experiences in war-torn Europe. He and other war-weary Black men were looking beyond the battlefields and focusing on their families and their uncertain futures. Nothing was promised to them after they had survived the purgatory of a clearly defined global conflagration.

Cynically, the idea of a war to end all wars was the genesis of perpetual war theory that materialized from the phrase "military industrial complex" coined by World War II general and hero, President Dwight David Eisenhower. He knew very well the power and the overwhelming influence a fraction of the business community had on the government's financial resources. Political ambition mixed with a gross appetite for money is a toxic combination.

President Eisenhower warned the nation before leaving the White House to beware of the military industrial complex because he foreshadowed the power and access to resources that collective had to influence the priorities and decisions of politicians. The accuracy of his prediction is impossible to overstate.

From World War II to the Korean War to Vietnam, to Cambodia, to Iraq, to Iran, to Syria, to Pakistan, to El Salvador, to Nicaragua, to Honduras, to the Philippines, to the secret and not-so-secret wars perpetuated around the world—including the inner-city drug wars across the United States—endless warfare is a multi-trillion dollar enterprise without limits but with the excessive cost of lives and extreme access to public resources that extend the reality of purgatory to all corners of the world.

The escalation of the Vietnam War in 1968 coincided with my conversion from a young and committed national warrior to a pacifist who had been exposed to Quakers and a very different way of life. The transformation began a mere two days after graduating high school. My hopes of attending the U.S. Naval Academy had been shattered when I failed the medical examination. The two-day process put me through the rigors of a military exercise of agility and physical ability. Although my athletic body endured the routines, my medical history and new discoveries washed me out.

Doctors at the Naval Hospital discovered that, in addition to my history with asthma, I had a heart murmur, allergy to wool, flat feet, and minor intolerances. Combined in the highly competitive entrance process, my long-held desire ended. Depression replaced elation.

The long course of my desire from junior high school to just weeks before high school graduation was finished. That's when Miss Bryant, my high school counselor, intervened and helped to set me on a course I have followed since learning about the American Friends Service Committee.

The new journey began with a meeting in the office of Kelly Brady, a member of the Los Angeles County Human

Relations Commission. I had known Kelly for a couple years. As the student body president and editor of our high school newspaper, Kelly and I had met several times before Miss Bryant arranged our conversation. Without any information or hints as to why Miss Bryant wanted me to talk to Kelly, she set up an appointment at his office in the Los Angeles County Administration Building a few weeks before my graduation. It was a sunny spring afternoon in Southern California the day Kelly and I met. Although Kelly and I knew each other from a variety of activities sponsored by our high school, our meeting in his office had nothing to do with the county or public service.

Miss Bryant had primed Kelly about my situation and the lost opportunity to attend the Naval Academy. Kelly and I had never discussed his personal life, including his attitude about the Vietnam War, the military, or my desire to attend the academy. What emerged from our meeting in his office remains for me a source of awe and profound impact.

Kelly began our conversation by talking about Quakers and pacifism. Although I had read about Quakers in our history books, I never gave much thought about them, and I never related any part of my life, faith, or ambition to them. My ignorance was openly evident.

Kelly talked about a program that was scheduled to begin two days after my high school graduation. It was sponsored by the American Friends Service Committee and would take up most of the summer. At that point, I had not applied to college, although I had been offered a scholarship to Stanford University. My focus on the Naval Academy was my only real desire. The Quaker project Kelly presented would propel my life in a very different direction. Amid listening to his proposal, my mind began to spin in a strange direction. My profound ignorance began running wildly. First, I thought Quakers were only dead white people in history books. It never occurred to me they were a very active religious sect still in existence. The second major surprise to me came as Kelly explained he, too, was a Quaker. He was neither dead nor white. He was a middle-aged Black man sitting at his office desk inviting me to consider working with the Quakers that summer.

How was a Black kid from Hollywatts supposed to make such a radical mental adjustment in real time and respond to an opportunity that only seconds ago was nonexistent and beyond the scope of my imagination? Miss Bryant had walked the long road with me from beginning to end. As my high school counselor, she knew me in ways I could not explain or had known. I was a child who lived in the promised land, as our community was called by our high school football coaches. Vietnam was purgatory as the body bags began arriving in our neighborhood. Our schoolmates, childhood friends, and older brothers had served their country in an inexplicable war, and my turn to serve was coming up.

The journey into pacifism was deliberate and steady. Exposure to the Quakers was a deep step toward that transformation in my life, but it did not come easily or readily. Although my childhood desire to join the navy was dulled, it was not destroyed. At least, not immediately. The transition from war sympathizer to pacifist required extensive reading, conscious listening, and disturbing reflection. The foundation of my life was grounded in service to my country. My father had been in the Navy during World War II. My next-door neighbor had served in that same war and remained in the military and advanced as a career officer. My community was patriotic. Our fathers had given their blood and now their sons were giving their lives in the Vietnam War. I was living beyond the realm of intellectual discourse. I was in a whirlwind of mental, moral, spiritual, and intellectual turmoil. Indeed, the journey into pacifism was not easy.

Many years later, as I reflected on those times, it occurred to me that my father was visibly supportive of my military ambition, but in the quietude of personal prayer and social awareness, he wanted a very different path for his son. He had been in the theater of war and that was not his desire for me, his only male offspring.

He never discouraged me. He walked with me. But I sensed his innermost conflict was being there for me while knowing too much about the reality he had lived and nearly died during World War II. Memories of the past informed his perspectives of the present.

The war in Vietnam was overheating with extreme violence. Inner-city youth were becoming fodder in the jungles of that distant nation. We knew very little about its history and its people. "Viet Cong" was a term used to identify the enemy. They were not people. They were a roving menace in a distant place who were reported in the nightly news and morning newspaper.

A MOTHER'S TEARS

Moaning
Groaning
No Articulation
Just Pain
Tears Crawling
Cheek to Chin
Huge and Hot
Like Summer Rain
Silent
Screams
Nobody Listens
Pleading
Cruel Voices at a Distance
Police
Monsters
Victims
Innocent
Her Only Child Is Dead
Nobody Cares

In the Pit of Her Soul
Empty
Like Easter's Tomb
Gaping Hole
Nothing Can Fill

Seven

I stepped happily off my flight from Cleveland Hopkins Airport that had landed smoothly and on time at Los Angeles International Airport. No air pockets or bumps across the dark skies spanning America's flyover Heartland. Such travel had become a familiar way of life that brought me home from my offices in Ohio and New York. Crisscrossing the country had become routine. That year, I had traveled nationally and internationally so often that I slept in my own bed at home for only seventy-five nights.

My job with the United Church Board for World Ministries, the humanitarian arm of a US-based denomination, allowed me to travel over oceans and continents several times a month. Boarding airplanes at night and flying from east to west after a full day at my New York or Cleveland offices meant huffing to airports, racing around parking lots, and passing through security checkpoints.

That was a regimen reserved for a veteran traveler who could precisely pinpoint each minute it took to complete the pre-board process and catch a plane on time to reach their destination.

Walking through my old neighborhood, memories of days in the past flooded my mind, pierced my heart, and seared my soul. Arriving home in that ever-quiet pocket of Hollywatts felt comfortable and peaceful. I still believed it had remained a protective enclave from the chaotic rhythm that defined international ministry and my side job as an occasional news reporter and radio talk show host. The changes that had occurred over the years could not be denied, but the soft glow of bedroom lamps shadowed through draped windows in our neighbors' homes was a reminder that civility had not been completely lost. There were hints of calm behind closed, locked doors.

Stepping from the back seat of the taxi onto my street caused me to think more deeply about how our once-tranquil neighborhood had changed. The cab driver had accepted my charge and drove me east of the Harbor Freeway from the airport on a Friday night.

Although the name, South Central Los Angeles, had been shortened to only "South L.A." in an imaginary expansion of our section of the vast metropolis, not all the changes that had taken place since my youth were bad.

There was greater diversity of cultures, languages, and cuisines across the great expanse of the Los Angeles Basin.

Dressed in my Southern California young professional attire of denim jeans, button-down collared shirt, and soft Reebok walking shoes, I threw my Tumi backpack over my shoulder, grabbed by single rollaway luggage from the trunk of the cab, and began the slow, short stroll up the sidewalk to the front door of my family's home on the corner of our street.

A quiet Friday night in Carver Manor was strangely different from my earliest memories when the sounds of live music defined our community. The absence of beats and taps by skilled fingers across the skins of well-honed bongos and other percussions reminded me how our way of life had once been good and keenly protected. The noiseless night now meant a formerly thriving neighborhood was on the verge of transitioning into a less familiar place.

The changes were not only external as I carried the appearance of a stranger from a distant place who shunned the briefcase for the more popular backpack slung over my shoulder. I was dressed to reflect a different style and reality that existed beyond the boundaries of Hollywatts and Carver Manor. I was a son coming home to bind the ties that united family, neighbors, and high expectations. Tomorrow's sunrise would allow me to fully see how much time and circumstances beyond the reach or control of my neighbors had changed what I previously knew so well.

I arose early the next day on a quiet Saturday morning to begin my walk through our neighborhood. Each step was a deliberate stride as I moved slowly, observing, listening, and smelling life. Almost immediately I glanced to my right and looked across the street, where two young children were running down the steps of a front porch as a middle-aged woman quickly followed them and called their names in a somewhat annoyed tone.

"Don't act like y'all grown and trying to get ahead of me," she was shouting above a whisper but not so loudly as to disturb the quietness of our street. Wilma Clackman never left home or ventured too far from our street. She first became pregnant when she was twelve years old.

We were the same age and good friends. Her boyfriend, Danny, lived around the corner and was one of the funniest people I knew. They had two children together as teenagers before he was gunned down and murdered. Young in age, Wilma and Danny grew old early in life.

The sounds on our street in the early days had been punctuated by swaying palm trees at sunset on Friday afternoons. We danced to the thumping rhythm of drums heard from house to house. People on our street would retreat from a week of labor and stretches of absent mothers, grandmothers, daughters, and sisters who spent too much of their lives away in homes across town working as the help to families who were not their own.

Fathers, uncles, sons, and brothers would come back home from daily jobs that did not define them, but merely provided the means for them to support their loved ones. The drums called to us and welcomed us back together. The drums signaled revelry. They were the beats of our neighborhood, and every weekend they sounded the unity that touched each of us within our community.

Walking down the street where I lived sent my thoughts back to a time when I was about the age of the children who were running from their house with their young grandmother in tow.

I used to practice scissor jumping and spinning from our porch over the hedges and landing without stopping as I dashed from my house to the corner store. I had no fear of hurting myself by tripping or falling. I raced to the store a block away that provided me a destination and purpose. It was quick and convenient for me to pick up some food for my grandmother to fix breakfast in the morning or prepare dinner in the afternoon.

Our house was where our friends and neighbors congregated to play and hang out. That was back during a time now locked in the distant past that used to be filled with memories and sacred moments. On this Saturday morning, as I began my stroll before my neighbors were fully aroused, I realized many of the people I once knew had moved away and were replaced by people I did not know. I had not seen some of my neighbors in several years after I moved away and out of the state. During that time, some of us had lost touch. But on the street where I had lived neighbors were still neighbors whether newly arrived or long-term residents.

Fannie and Willie Thomas lived two houses from us, directly across the street from the Clackman's home. Mother and Daddy Thomas, as we called them, were my godparents. Like my father and mother, they had moved to Los Angeles from Memphis, Tennessee.

They were devout Baptists. Deacon Thomas, as he was known, was a member of St. Paul's Baptist Church on Figueroa about six miles from our street. Every Sunday, he drove passed what seemed like hundreds of other Baptist churches to reach his own church home.

Mother Thomas was a member of the Missionary Society, a group of women who would attend to the needs of people all over Los Angeles who were sick or shut in. She would make hospital and home visits. The fortunate patients were nearly always treated to her full-face smile and the warmth of her big heart. On occasion, she would add something incredibly special for patients as she delivered one of her homemade sweet potato pies or coconut cakes.

Unlike most of the men on our street, Daddy Thomas was not a military veteran. Instead, he had spent the war years doing hard labor as a civilian in Memphis. He was, in fact, a different kind of veteran and survivor.

He fled the threats of daily lynchings and brutal assaults on Black men and women in the lingering Confederacy. After arriving safely in South Central Los Angeles, he successfully landed a job outside Dixie at a steel mill, but now he was in a city that rivaled Southern hostility and segregation so familiar in almost every aspect, including the racially divided housing sections of Los Angeles.

"I hated white people," the pious deacon once confided to me. "I'd seen too much of what they were capable of doing and more than willing to do to hurt and kill Black folk."

The pain mixed with anger in his voice seared a memory that confounded what I thought I had understood and had come to know about my godfather. He was a simple but complex man who kept his weary soul tucked away deeply in the reservoir of his soul. He had never shown or projected hatred toward anyone and, yet, in a tender moment he unraveled a web of sadness and anger.

The passing of time and an unforgettable incident transformed his view of white people in the world. It was an unexpected moment that blurred the past and cleared the path toward a future that had eluded him and seemed unimaginable from his experiences in the American South. The change catapulted his heart, mind, and soul. It transformed his outlook on the world.

Our neighbors knew the possibilities and consequences whenever they found themselves in a strange place alone across town. It didn't require a lot of detail or creative imagination to remind them of episodes when marauders appeared and created a crisis. It was never lost on any of our neighbors that we lived in a post-military, but true Southern neighborhood.

Daddy Thomas was aware of deadly situations that attracted the attention of gun-happy police officers who searched for any sudden movement; or an incident spied by the unfortunate arrival of a malicious white man who could change an inconvenience into a tragic set of circumstances that could quickly, easily, and without provocation result in sudden death or critical injury. In almost every such incident involving a Black man and police officers, such an act was ruled "justifiable" by prosecutors who were cohorts in the social conspiracy to keep the peace by any means necessary.

Being stranded in the middle of the night on almost any street in Los Angeles did, in fact, pose a dangerous hazard for anyone—particularly Black men. Death and madness crept on tip toes from a variety of sources, including cops, marauders, gangs, and criminally insane prowlers.

Brain-dead thugs with no desire to let other people live were maniacal night crawlers who availed themselves of sudden disaster. They could instantaneously alter an innocent person's future. They were misguided men who roamed dark streets.

"One night while I was going to work," Daddy Thomas explained, "my car broke down in the middle of the street. It was during a heavy, downpouring rainstorm, and I didn't quite know what to do in that wet darkness," he said.

"I got out of my car," Daddy Thomas continued, "and I started to push it to the side of the road. I was steering with my right hand and buckling my legs with my toes bending forward to give me enough lift to get traction and move my car to the curb. Suddenly, I noticed lights from a vehicle coming toward me. The rain was really coming down," Daddy Thomas's voice turned raspy as he retold me the details of his story.

"A truck followed me to the side of the road," Daddy Thomas remembered, "and the driver got out. He was a white man. I didn't know quite what to do. I didn't have my pistol and nobody else was around," Daddy Thomas slowly released each word.

"Hey, mister, can I help you?" the white driver shouted as he stepped out of his truck and walked toward Daddy Thomas.

"My car just stopped running," Daddy Thomas responded.

"Well, what do you think is wrong?" the stranger asked, as his soaking wet clothes dripped in the torrent.

"I don't know. I've got plenty of gas. It just stopped," Daddy Thomas said.

"I tell you what, why don't we push your car a couple blocks up the street?" the white stranger offered. "There's a service station that's still open. We can at least take it there and probably leave it if the mechanic is already gone," the stranger suggested.

Daddy Thomas felt confused by the courtesy, and his sufficient exposure to Southern whites made this white man seem curiously different. Daddy Thomas hesitated before he pushed aside a stubborn, well-seasoned response. The rain, darkness, dead car, and a seemingly non-threatening white man flooded his senses.

"Good," Daddy Thomas finally decided. "Thank you!"

After describing to me this story about getting unexpected help that did not require a hassle, he told me it resulted in a profound change in his life.

"I hated white people," Daddy Thomas repeated with emphasis. "I never thought I would ever feel differently about them. But that night that one white man showed me something that I could not believe was possible. He was a white man who helped me, a Black man, and he went out of his way in the cold, hard-pounding rain," he recalled.

"Every day I still pray to God for the strength to love everybody, no matter if they are Black, white, pink or purple," he went on in a tone that elevated to a sermonic pitch.

As a deacon in his church, Daddy Thomas was the epitome of God's enduring mercy and neighborly love for all humankind. He possessed a guilt that caused him to purge his old feelings of hatred toward white people by helping anyone who needed his assistance.

There were no criteria or tests a person had to pass to receive Daddy Thomas's aid. Only Mother Thomas matched his distribution of boundless gifts and humane presence. Together, they formed a team of extreme kindness that was extended to anyone who needed help. The Clackman, Thomas, and Cribbs families were neighbors who helped to teach and show me how to overcome prejudice by offering a hand to anyone who needed help or who came into my view and obviously required assistance.

But real help always began at home and spread across the street and throughout our neighborhood. In fact, our fledgling community depended on something far more precious than money to survive.

As homeowners, of course, people and families on our street had jobs and money. But what helped all of us get by and made it possible for most of us to get by was the bartering system. Our neighbors exchanged services instead of money. That was a particularly good thing for our family. My daddy went to work every day at Los Angeles County General Hospital. He was a janitor and foreman in the housekeeping department. He got up at the same time early every morning and was out of our house by six o'clock to be at his job on time at seven.

My mother woke up every morning at five o'clock and left home at seven on her way to McDonnell Douglas Aircraft plant in Santa Monica. Together, my parents earned about nine thousand dollars a year. Whatever the income, my parents took great pride in being homeowners. If their income didn't put them in the middle class, their morality and mentality placed their values as middle class.

My father was also skilled as an automotive mechanic. Around the corner, our neighbor, Mr. Barber, worked on radios and television sets. Another neighbor, Mr. Allison, was a certified public accountant who helped to prepare our parents' taxes every year. Up the street from our house was Deacon Riles, a plumber. And across the street from him lived Deacon Holloway, who was an electrician.

Whenever a member of the community had a need, neighbors would come together and help each other. It was not always about making money and boosting business. We were neighbors, and neighbors help each other any way they can and whenever they are needed.

There was another family on the street where I lived, the Kingsleys, who had converted their garage into a lounge for late night entertainment. They were fun-loving, partying people.

One day, their daughter, Betty Jane, my older sister, Dellena, and I created a musical trio. The Kingsleys' lounge was perfect for our newly formed band, and it became the scene for our musical sets.

Betty Jane played the drums, Dellena played the piano, and I played the upright string bass. We would jam for hours, composing music and filling up our time with jazz, blues, gospel, and our original compositions. It was our safe place to hang out and hone our musical skills. Music was the ever-present, consistent, and persistent daily play and environmental element that permeated our block.

Around the corner from our house and up the street from the Kingsleys, Mr. and Mrs. Allison provided space for the congas, bongos, and drummers to congregate every Friday to spread the news and beat the sounds that carried through the air and wafted into the sky. That is how we lived in our neighborhood, George Washington Carver Manor. We played our soundtrack of salvation, safety, and sanity for our neighbors and everybody to hear.

RICH AND GOOD

Our souls were rich
Not dead in a ditch
Sewing us back into a single stitch
Strong and alive
We did more than survive
To overcome their racist jive
Our parents' love
Felt like a glove
Beaming down from heaven above
Words and schemes
Couldn't destroy our dreams
Or turn our whispers into screams
Life was real good
In our neighborhood
And we did all that we could
We turned back the lies
And never despised
Those who came in human disguise

EIGHT

I continued to walk in front of houses now occupied by faces and names unknown and unfamiliar. The intent of retaining the original aspirations of men, women, and families who sought to discover greater opportunities still appeared evident more than seventy years after the homes were originally constructed.

Death had taken its toll as the number of original residents who remained dwindled. From house to house I recognized their faces and genuine friendliness. But they had become survivors who lived more indoors than outside. I easily recalled their family names: Smith, Walters, Johnson, Miles, Yancy, Harper, Anderson, Dodd, Tyler, Aaron, Reynolds, Webster, Tinsdale, Haswell, Hughes, Warington, Uriah, Caswell, Buttress, Darrington, Pilson, Paris, Markham, Kilgore, Tipson, Chase, Aspen, White, Bales, Jones, Murphy, Davidson, Dyson, Chamberland,

Wilson, Lewis, Black, Carroll, Moran, Ludlow, Blackwall, Morrison, Walton, Gordon, Stewart, Pruitt, Madison, Biltmore, Love, Norman, Cribbs.

Taking a stroll on the street where I once lived and my family still resides reminded me of the community functions that were created by our parents: the Ajalon Temple of Truth Baptist Church located up the street from my house and the Southern Area Boys Club—the center of social activities and public gatherings in our neighborhood. As I walked pass that former citadel of male pride and prowess, there was more than a significant name change. Now, our former afterschool retreat had been renamed the Watts-Willowbrook Boys and Girls Club. It appeared progress had been made over the years with the long overdue extension of opportunities once reserved for "boys only."

When the Boys Club originally opened, I could not wait to turn seven years old and become eligible to go inside and participate as a member. Separated by a chain-linked fence that surrounded George Washington Carver Elementary School, the Boys Club was off limits to the youngest boys in our neighborhood, along with girls of any age.

On occasion, girls and younger boys were invited to attend specific events that were open to the whole community. But to take advantage of the wide array of sports, games, arts and crafts, camps, field trips, and other numerous daily activities offered inside the new structure and its athletic field, a boy had to be at least seven years old.

Indeed, it was a glorious day on my seventh birthday when I raced out of school and ran straight inside the Boys Club to sign up for membership. The aroma upon entry indicated the Boys Club was where the action took place. The floors shined clean. Pool tables lined the large activity room across from the entrance desk. There was a library to the left of the front door, and the administration office was to the right. Past the administration office and straight down the hall was the gymnasium, where a group of older and bigger boys were playing a basketball game.

Turning seven years old was my key to heaven on earth. Vertis Hayes ran the arts and crafts center. An accomplished artist, Mr. Hayes already had made tremendous artistic contributions at historic Black universities, museums, and art galleries in the South and in New York City. When he arrived in Los Angeles, his passion and creative mind provided gifts of wonder and beauty for every boy who entered his palace of artistic expressions.

Mr. Hayes offered many different opportunities to inspire us to apply our imagination. He taught us how to transform plastic string into necklaces and jewelry; turn plain paper into masterpieces; wood block into furniture; and mounds of clay into crockery. Whatever a young boy's mind might conceive of, Mr. Hayes knew how to turn it into a tangible object.

Bill Sims, Al Chism, and James Rodgers ran the Boys Club's sports activities with a team of dedicated men and women who offered their services at minimum costs to the children.

Parents and families came every day to take advantage of the many opportunities offered by the Boys Club.

On the outside wall at the entrance to the Southern Area Boys Club was a placard that acknowledged the financial support from the Los Angeles Times Foundation that helped to make it available to our neighborhood.

In addition to ping pong, pool, arts and crafts, the library, and basketball, the Boys Club organized baseball, football, track, and boxing teams. The boxing team appeared on KHJ-TV, a local Los Angeles television station, that aired a program called "Kid Gloves." Years later, I went to work at KHJ-TV, where I launched my television news career. The call letters to the station were changed to KCAL-TV.

The athletic teams at the Southern Area Boys Club competed against other Boys Clubs in Los Angeles County, San Diego, Riverside, and throughout Southern California. We even went to Las Vegas and played against that city's championship baseball team. The Boys Club also sponsored chess and checker tournaments. The room that attracted my attention was the library, where we could read, study, and enhance ourselves academically.

Like the rest of our community, the Boys Club did not have a swimming pool. In fact, my grandmother led a campaign to bring the first public swimming pool to Hollywatts. It was situated at Will Rogers Park (later renamed Watkins Park after Mr. Ted Watkins, who founded the Watts Labor Community Action Committee).

Members of the Boys Club competed in the Junior Olympics. Our team won first place in several events, including the 440-yard relay. I was the first leg on the relay team. Along with Bill and Jim, there was Mr. Culpepper (Pepper), Mr. Mills, Claude Williams, Obie Jones, Oscar Love, Chris Harpole, and a staff of volunteers who dedicated their time to serving the boys and young men in our neighborhood.

In addition to sports and playtime, the Boys Club provided field trips to theaters and an array of cultural centers. It brought celebrities to our community, including boxing heavyweight champions Muhammad Ali and Archie Moore, along with actors and entertainers.

The person who stood out to me the most was Mr. Stan Sanders. He had attended Oxford University as a Rhodes Scholar and had grown up in our community. Mr. Sanders was an attorney and local legend. His brilliance and social justice orientation inspired every part of me.

He was my public idol. He was down to earth and got down to business when it came to defending the integrity of our community. Stan Sanders inspired me to adopt a phrase that my best friend, Chris Harpole, coined: "I am a proud product of Watts, Willowbrook, and Compton."

Several times a year, the Boys Club opened its doors and allowed girls to enter and watch movies, hold holiday parties, celebrate Halloween, and attend neighborhood dances.

The Boys Club was a very special place for families. My parents, for example, rented the Boys Club for their twenty-fifth wedding anniversary. It was the hub for various occasions to meet the social needs of people throughout our community.

It was the fertile ground on which my entry into Black manhood and social expectations were planted and launched. Excellence was always expected. At the same time, there were unsponsored events that took place in the back of the bus during field trips or in unattended spaces where cultural ploys like playing the "Dozens" took place.

The "Dozens" was a game conducted among boys to show their prowess by out-disrespecting each other's mother in crude, comedic exhibitions of verbal assaults. The winner was determined by a boy's ability to say the harshest, most despicable characterization of someone's mother without exhaustion. The loser was either the guy who ran out of terrible things to say about somebody else's mother or the one who cried or wanted to fight because he lacked the ability to hurl a harsher slur as a comeback. It was not a game for wimps, cowards, or anyone who exhibited bad sportsmanship.

The Boys Club also sponsored my first camping experience at Big Bear Lake in Southern California. That week-long adventure away from my family occurred when I was nine years old. It broadened my worldview and etched a lasting impression on what it meant to be a man and to commit myself to making real contributions to improve conditions in the larger society.

While the Southern Area Boys Club offered a strong platform for young men, the women and mothers in our community felt the vacancy of coordinated activities for their daughters. So, my mother and a group of women in our neighborhood decided to create a place for girls.

The "Little Ladies Club" was formed, and my older sister, Dellena, became one of its first members. She joined daughters around our community in creating an organization that focused on the needs and development of young women. They began recruiting by going house to house surveying and inviting other girls to join them. In short order, they had many girls excited about creating their own club.

Their next challenge was to find someplace where they could hold their own weekly meetings. They solicited the support of fathers and other men to help subsidize their efforts and provide transportation. While I don't know what exactly the girls did inside the Little Ladies Club, they invited families, including boys, to join them one summer when they went camping at Joshua Tree, a desert community in Southern California near Palm Springs.

The Little Ladies Club offered instructions on how girls and young ladies should conduct themselves in public, how to plan their future with an emphasis on education and proper training for employment, and how to carry themselves as women in society. Dellena was so encouraged by the Little Ladies Club that she became a leader at school and developed greater confidence. At all times, the girls were expected to present themselves as competent, respectful, and committed contributors to society by uplifting the values and ideals of strong Black women and to always perform as Little Ladies.

While the Southern Area Boys Club and the Little Ladies Club had a great influence on how I grew up, there were three foundational institutions that reinforced my fundamental African American values: my church, my schools, and my family.

Transported from both the rural and urban South, an unambiguous set of tenets came with our neighbors who built houses of worship, taught in our schools, and raised their children and families in Carver Manor. For the children, every adult had the authority to correct our behavior if we demonstrated an ounce of deviation from the norms delineated in our homes.

There were expectations that the dreams of our parents would be realized as we matured and began to take on the responsibilities of adulthood. Every adult and child had a role to play to ensure the future would be brighter and better than the past. There were very clear and specific reasons our parents had left the Deep South. Through their determination and religious fervor, my family and our neighbors wanted to ensure their children were guarded and protected from outside influences that could jeopardize in any way their intentional efforts to create conditions and opportunities for our success. We were continually instructed about our purpose as human beings and American citizens. We were taught we had an obligation to work hard and do better than our parents in whatever field we chose for ourselves.

As our community in Carver Manor was being populated by new arrivals, men like my grandfather were among the work crew who helped to construct the local house of worship, Ajalon Temple of Truth Missionary Baptist Church. It was erected directly two blocks from our home, and we could look out our front window and watch the white building going up on the corner.

Our neighbors made up the congregation of Ajalon, which soon became the sacred gathering place for more than worship. It was used to bring people up to date on issues from across the country. Our pastor, the Rev. Dr. George W. Bell, led trips to Africa, Yosemite National Park, and all over the nation. My grandmother was the president of the Pastor's Aid Society, a team that made sure he had everything he needed to execute his ministry.

The church was the center of our family's life. Sunday was a time to give reverence to God. Church began in the morning with Sunday School at 9:30 and worship service at eleven o'clock; afternoon service with visiting churches started at 3:30 and was followed with a meal. The Baptist Young People Union (BYPU), later called Baptist Training Union (BTU), began in the evening at six o'clock and was designed to teach children and young adults how to conduct themselves in a Christian manner. The day ended with night service that started at 7:30. It was a full day of religious education, worship, and spiritual development.

Tuesday night was Bible study for deacons and persons preparing for ministry; Wednesday night was when the church held its weekly prayer meeting; Thursday night was reserved for adult choir rehearsal. Saturday was the day focused on youth recreation and hosting activities in the church parking lot—which was used exclusively for roller skating.

Every year on the Fourth of July, the men of the church traveled across town to East Los Angeles and set up at Lincoln Park for the annual picnic. They would arrive at the park very early in the morning to secure the covered area and fire up the barbecue pits. My grandmother oversaw the ice cream that was both homemade and store bought. Her favorite were the pink coconut bars that she purchased directly from the manufacturer on Central Avenue near Fifty-Fourth Street.

God, family, and community were the priorities taught in the church, home, and at school. Our pastor was the Rev. Dr. George W. Bell. He was a biblical scholar who focused on the African presence in the Bible. He led trips to the Holy Land with an emphasis on the Black cultures and dark-skinned people in Palestine, Egypt, and the Middle East. His central message focused on the intentional placement of God's people throughout history and our responsibility to love God, love one another, and to protect the Earth. He delved into the abuse of God's name and the vile corruption of Jesus's teachings that produced and developed the slave trade and the exploitation of Africa and the reckless disregard of her people for vile profit.

Many of our schoolteachers also lived in our neighborhood and attended local and nearby churches. They shared the same religious fervor our parents possessed and held the same reverence for God that was instilled in us from an early age. If the church was established to heal and strengthen our souls, the schools were built to sharpen our minds. Both were instructional institutions to make sure we were well-grounded and prepared for whatever the world had to offer.

George Washington Carver Elementary School was one of five elementary schools in our Hollywatts school district. It was developed to serve the residents of Hollywatts in Carver Manor and Palm Lane, a public housing development community located directly across Compton Avenue from our home. Just north of our neighborhood in Carver Manor were homes and ranches where other children lived who attended our school. Their homes were older than our newly built houses in Carver Manor, and they retained the original rural atmosphere alongside the emerging urban sprawl. Many of them had horses and cattle. They were and remain true cowboys who have gained national and international fame.

In addition to Carver, our elementary school district included Lincoln, Willowbrook (later renamed John F. Kennedy), Ralph Bunche, and Marian Anderson. Carver offered a comprehensive music program for singers and musicians. Dellena sang in our school choir and performed in front of Ms. Marian Anderson, who attended the dedication ceremony of the school opening that was named in her honor. Mrs. Anderson had been denied an opportunity to sing at an event sponsored by the patriotic organization, Daughters of the American Revolution, earlier in her esteemed career in 1939. Twenty years later, she was recognized for her courage and excellent vocal skills. The fifth elementary school in our district honored her life with her name and she came to witness the honor of her recognition.

The Carver Elementary School music program was led by Vincent Gomez, a twenty-three-year-old violinist and bass player, who eventually became my mentor and friend.

Vince was a jazz musician who performed in Hollywood at night and commuted to our neighborhood every day to work with children. In addition to Vince taking the school choir to sing at the Marian Anderson Elementary School's opening, he took his young students to the Los Angeles County Fair to display their musical talents. They also visited the home of then Vice President Richard Nixon, where members of the choir met his mother at her home in Whittier, California. Vince directed our elementary school choir as they performed in front of her.

Vince grew up in San Francisco in a Filipino family. He proudly identified himself as Filipino American and made a distinction between his parents who migrated to the United States from the Philippines and himself since he was born in this country. His job with our elementary school district of teaching Black children came at a very critical time in his life. He was raising his young daughter as a single parent and working two jobs. He told me many years later that the opportunity to teach voice and instruments to Black kids in Hollywatts helped him survive what had become an otherwise difficult period. We were his Black saviors.

While Dellena was singing in the Carver choir, I learned how to play bass. I wanted to play drums, but Vince convinced me to learn a string instrument. He said, "You can learn to play the drums later." Over the years, our lives would continue to connect and intermingle at different times and in many different places.

During my high school years, Vince and I came together at the annual National Conference of Christians and Jews Brotherhood Camp. Later, our paths crossed again following the assassinations of San Francisco Mayor George Moscone and Supervisor Harvey Milk. Vince had gone to school with Mayor Moscone.

Our lives continued to crisscross in various situations, including when we began working together on projects throughout Southern California with undocumented immigrants. Vince had developed a program that inspired people to write about their life stories. They could write poetry or prose. The poems were transcribed into songs and that music was taught to them. Vince then changed people who previously had never sung into singers. He created choirs where they performed in public concerts and they sang their own poems that were transposed into music.

I would eventually joke with him by saying, "Vince, you know, we kids in Hollywatts saved your life. And I'm the bad penny who keeps turning up."

Many of the teachers who were also our neighbors shared the same values and desires of our parents for our success as citizens and productive participants in society. Some of us attended the same church. Thus, church, school, and the family were intertwined in a commitment to produce the best and earn a place of respect in a country that denied the full extent of our humanity. No matter how much we did to demonstrate our loyalty, our family and neighbors were never fully appreciated for the sacrifices they made for an ungrateful nation.

We were the promised land kids surviving the dangers of purgatory.

SUBLIMINAL GENOCIDE

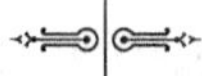

Hallelujah, come to Glory
Hear a riddle and this story
Young and old don't matter a wit
Everyone's invited to play this skit
Subliminal Genocide
Look into the mirror
What do I see
Dark colored white mask
Staring back at me
Ghost of a person
Dead standing up
Subliminal Genocide
Somebody go tell it
Make somebody scream
We are all going down
And this ain't no dream
Subliminal Genocide
One way or the other
It's coming for you

Fake it or make it
Illusions do come true
Life is its enemy
You are its prey
Locked in your soul
The answers always wait
Subliminal Genocide
That's what it is
Causing you to curse
That blessed day
When your mother screamed
And gave you birth

Nine

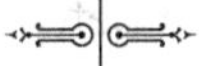

Carver Manor sat in a field of diversity. It was a Black and Brown residential area where English and Spanish intermingled. It wasn't until I moved to work in Reno, Nevada, did I learn that many of the people I thought were Mexicans were actually Native Americans whose ancestry was Indigenous and dated back more than 7,000 years on the lands where our neighborhood was built. It was only after I started reporting on the Inter-Tribal Council of Northern Nevada that I began to learn about the Gabrielino-Tongva Tribe.

The blatant theft of their lands was made more disgusting by the insulting meager court-ordered assessment and compensation of seven cents per acre from which the court deducted administration costs. Many of the Native Americans around us were also veterans of World War II who had made great sacrifices for a country that failed to honor them and used every deception to steal their lands and scrub away their existence.

For me to fully grasp what my eyes were witnessing on my street, I had to learn more about the people who had lived on the land long before any of our migrant families moved to Hollywatts. The intentional displacement and removal of many Native Americans living on more than 64 million acres dated back to the mid-1800s. That new insight taught me about the determined, designed plans that changed our community by the unseen shenanigans devised in the demonic minds of monsters who preferred displacement of families and acquisition of money and land much more than human life.

The Gabrielino-Tongva Tribe resided on the vast Southland that extended from the Sierra Nevada Mountain range to the Pacific Ocean. Although I had lived on their lands my whole life, I knew nothing about the ancestral owners. The arbitrary Mexico-United States border erected at San Ysidro just south of San Diego cuts through Indigenous homelands. It has forced the separation and displacement of families who still have relatives living on both sides of that relatively new border. Their removal resulted in climate change that shocked the environment and continues to affect the seasons. It is almost unfathomable to imagine the harm and the gross extent of suffering their ancestors endured. The historical record is clear and unambiguous about the genocide perpetrated on a gentle, life-loving people who were generous and welcomed the unsuspected monstrous, murdering invaders who returned kindness with untold deadly force.

The cruel reality is that Native Americans, who cared for the land, were slaughtered at an estimated rate of 56 million people over a 300-year period following the arrival of Christopher Columbus in 1492. That is according to researchers at University College in London. While there are disputes about the actual number of deaths, the evidence of cultures destroyed, people removed from their homelands, and the continuous denial of adequate compensation cannot be buried or denied. When coupled with the importation of other people, including African men, women, and children during the centuries of the legalized slave trade, the environmental and human transformation devastated land and humanity.

Many families who followed the road to the promised land in Hollywatts carried inside them mixed blood of Africans and Native Americans. They came from Oklahoma, Louisiana, Mississippi, Alabama, Tennessee, Florida, and the Heartland of the United States. They were Cherokee, Choctaw, Cree, Seminole, and descendants of those who were forcefully expelled on the "Trail of Tears."

Simply understood, our neighbors were survivors of World War II, and some were direct descendants of the century's long wars against Native Americans. They represented the hopes and promises of generations who suffered and endured the unimaginable travesties meted by the more recently arrived European settlers, whose very survival depended on the generous and more extravagant hospitality of their rescuers and first responders.

It is an act of complicity to dismiss or fail to include the continuing injustice against the Gabrielino-Tongva peoples who too often today remain invisibly present on their almost fully occupied ancestral homeland. Purgatory preceded the arrival of post–World War II veterans and their African American families in Carver Manor.

As I walked down the street where I lived, making those connections between the past and the present, my memories raced across time and territory.

I thought back to standing in a very long line in Hollywood outside the KTLA-TV studio on Sunset Boulevard waiting for a chance to interview for one of a handful of jobs in broadcasting. My girlfriend, Rachel Isaiah, made the trip with me. We watched people go in and come out of an office. Finally, my turn to go in arrived. Tad Dunbar, the news director of KOLO-TV in Reno, conducted the interview. Although I had worked in the newsroom at KHJ-TV that past summer as a news writer, my experience was scant at best.

"What took you so long?" Rachel asked me after I walked out the room.

"What do you mean," I asked.

"You went in there and stayed," she responded.

"Really?" I asked. "I just answered their questions."

"Everybody else went in and came out quickly," she continued. "You went in and didn't come right out," she said.

"I didn't realize I was in there very long," I told her.

About a week after that interview, I received a telephone call from Tad. He wanted to hire me to join his staff as a television news reporter. I was both surprised and thrilled. I accepted the job offer and then looked up Reno to see where it was located and to learn something about the city and the state of Nevada.

About six months after I started working at KOLO-TV, it was my very good fortune to meet members of the Shoshone, Paiute, and Washoe tribes at the Inter-Tribal Council of Northern Nevada.

After six consecutive weeks of going to the council's office every day in search of getting a lead or the opportunity to cover a story, my consistency finally began to pay off. I had endured rejections, dismissals, and being disregarded. Finally, I was referred to a VISTA (Volunteers in Service to America) worker at the far end of the urban reservation. There, I met Kathleen Sweeney, a dedicated, wide-eyed white woman, who was working with children.

"Hi, I'm Art Cribbs from KOLO-TV," I introduced myself.

"I know who you are," Kathleen responded. "Everybody knows you are the only Black television reporter in Reno and Northern Nevada."

"I was told you could help me with a story," I continued.

"What do you mean?" she asked. "I don't have a story for you."

"Well, I've been coming to the council every day for the past six weeks, and today I was told to see you." The words stumbled slowly from my mouth.

"I don't know what is going on that is newsworthy," Kathleen said in a surprised tone. "I just work with the kids here."

"Great," I said with as much excitement as I could muster.

"Are you kidding me?" she asked.

"No, not at all. What are you doing with the kids?" I probed.

"We are planning our powwow," Kathleen said, seemingly dismissing her own news.

Her words filled my mind with wandering images that were disconnected and foreign. I had heard the word, "powwow," somewhere but not with any clear significance. What was a powwow? The question was a powerful concoction, like a tonic that soothed the ache in my soul. After six weeks of seeking any hint of a possible story, Kathleen was about to introduce me to a culturally sacred ritual performed by children.

"When is the powwow?" I asked with mild enthusiasm.

The more significant question, "What is a powwow?" formed quickly in my head but never came out of my mouth.

"In a couple of days," the generous answer rushed into my ears.

"Where? What time?" I questioned with the excitement of a lottery winner.

"It's here on the Res at 7:30 Wednesday night." Kathleen had made my day.

Wednesday night felt slow in arriving. After weeks of being ignored, dismissed, and suspected of being a Black troublemaker or a news reporter ready to shine a negative light on Native Americans, I finally had a lead on a story. Kathleen had just handed me an authentic, true exposure to the precious, protected inner world of Native American children.

I arrived at the Inter-Tribal Council Community Center around 6:30, about an hour before the powwow was scheduled to begin. I set up my 16-millimeter Auricon camera and sound box, plugged an electric cord into a socket, and set up lights on the sides of the staging area. I had placed a full reel of film in the camera before I left the station. I was ready to record my first story on Reno and Washoe County's urban American Indians.

My first lesson was learning clocks and time are manufactured for inconvenience and annoyances by invaders who insisted on using the contrived invention of time to fulfill their own purposes. Among the residents on the reservation, time was at best an estimation of when activities would commence. Seven-thirty arrived and passed without any sounds or sense of starting the powwow. Eight-thirty and 9:30 also came and went without a drumbeat.

Closer to ten o'clock, the drumming finally began, and two lines of children in traditional Native American attire started dancing into the room. Proud and beautifully dressed, each child passed from the back, to the center aisle, and to the front of the room. The drummers provided the rhythm until the last child was in place.

It was too late to get the story on the air for that evening's eleven o'clock newscast. The next night, KOLO-TV aired the story as a human-interest feature. Those days trying to get any bit of a story finally paid off. The children's powwow was a real story that reflected the cultural values of the Native American people, and the love they held for their children. For some news people, it was a soft story. For the Inter-Tribal Council leaders, coverage of their children was the key that opened the gates of heaven. My visits to the reservation became my news beat. Stories about life among Northern Nevada Native Americans covered every genre of news and included a visit by Senator Ted Kennedy, who took a deep concern about water rights and protection, an issue that was of great concern among the tribes.

I owe the extended success of my career in television news to the Washoe, Shoshone, and Paiute people in Northern Nevada. One of the stories that shaped my career involved the Yomba Tribe about 200 miles northeast of Reno. For years, the reservation existed without electricity generated by the Sierra Pacific Power Company. The public utility diverted its power lines between Utah and Nevada in four directions around and away from the Native American reservation. Although it was more cost effective to run the lines to and through the reservation, Sierra Pacific intentionally denied them power.

John Buggs, a tribal leader from the Pyramid Lake Tribe, escorted me to Yomba. We drove across Northern Nevada in the dead cold of January to talk to the tribal leaders and residents at Yomba. In the middle of our drive, John asked me, "Art, what do you see?"

As I steered our car on the early morning road as the sun was rising, I declared, "Nothing! Just open space."

"Look again," John instructed.

"I still see nothing," I said. "What do you see?"

"Well," John responded deliberately, "I see food, water, and shelter. I can live and survive out here."

"Really?" I inquired. "You see all that out here in the open desert?"

"Young brother, this is my home. This is my people's land. This is where we live, and we survive here on Mother Earth. It has everything we need."

That was the second lesson taught to me about Native American life.

When we arrived at the Yomba reservation, a group of men was waiting for us. It was the first time a television news reporter had been on the reservation. John and I stepped away from the car. John spoke to the small gathering of men and introduced me. The sight of the men was most noticeable because a couple were standing in the cold morning air dressed in T-shirts without jackets or sweaters. It was twenty-two degrees, and snow covered the ground. Yet they were ready to take this young novice reporter on a tour of the reservation, which included the classrooms where students had already started their lessons.

I asked permission to shoot the classroom with the Auricon camera sitting on the car's back seat. I also brought the company's Bell and Howell silent camera that we called "the grinder" because of the loud grinding sound it made when in use. The students were curious about me both as a Black man and a newsman. Both identities appeared out of place. Slowly, one student walked toward me and asked to see the camera and if I would take his picture.

The ice was breaking that cool morning in a classroom that was slightly warmer than the chilly outdoors. Another student came over, and eventually more students followed. I asked them about the cold and how they tried to keep warm. The children were the first interviews I conducted about the lack of power and weathering the cold. The tribal leaders were successful in manufacturing heat to reduce the impact of Nevada's cold months. John explained how the utility company's determination to keep power away from the Yomba reservation cost its customers more money. "This diversion is paid for by the Sierra Pacific Power Company's users across the state," John said.

Once we returned to Reno, I went straight to work and developed the film. I began writing the story, editing the film, and preparing to tell our viewers about life at Yomba and the scheme executed by the Sierra Pacific Power Company. That was the story that set my career on an accelerated path. I owe my broadcast success to the Yomba reservation residents who weathered the cold winters and excessively hot summers without heaters and air conditioners. The public utility company was determined not to provide power to them. The people trusted me with telling their story, and that story eventually led to Sierra Pacific Power Company changing its policy and transmitting power directly through Yomba and continuing across Northern Nevada.

John asked me about Paiute and Shoshone people who lived near my home in Hollywatts. "No, I did not know any of them," I confessed with a hint of embarrassment. In fact, I was surprised to hear about any Native Americans anywhere near "our" promised land. John expressed his disappointment at my ignorance. The people he named were tribal leaders of longstanding communities. They were members of a people who had lived on their lands continually for centuries. I did not know them or their history and was not aware of any Native Americans where my family also had settled. That was lesson three.

WHAT WORLD ARE YOU IN

What world are you in
As the beat goes on
Time is ticking
Everyone's on the run
No thought is given
To the news of the day
Seems everybody's busy
Just wanting to play
Names unfamiliar
From places unknown
Dropping bombs on strangers
No thought or groan
Madness embraces us
There is no rest
Fighting for a cause
Without reason or a test
Fantasy and illusion
Presented like fact
Create scenarios

That knock us off track
Shut off the noise
Get real with a friend
Ask only one question
What world are you in?

TEN

Returning to the street where I lived after years of living in different cities across the United States brought back an assortment of memories. The outside of homes looked mostly unchanged, with their manicured lawns, neatly painted houses, and nice cars parked in driveways, but the streets were unfamiliarly quiet. There were no children playing outside. No sounds of beating drums traveling throughout the air. No neighbors waving and greeting each other. It was Saturday morning, and my street laid bare of human presence. It was an eerily shift in reality. New people had moved into some of the homes. The Miles's house was under construction and was having a second story built.

William Miles and his sister, Sharon, were my idols. They were smart and good looking. William was a journalist who worked for the *Compton Bee* newspaper. I read his articles religiously and copied his style of writing until I developed my own voice. He was my model news reporter. Whenever I asked him a question about a story or his thoughts on an issue, he always took the time to listen and share generously. He never turned me away or ignored me. He was always helpful and sometimes seemed genuinely interested in me. I credit William and my sister Dellena with putting me on a course to become a news reporter.

Mr. Miles, William's father, worked at the post office, while Mrs. Miles stayed home and took care of their children. Up the street from the Miles's home lived Mr. and Mrs. Harper. He also worked for the post office and had served in the United States Army as a sergeant. Mrs. Harper worked as a cashier at our local Safeway grocery store.

I spent many days in the Harpers' home listening to Mr. Harper's stories and his philosophy about honesty and responsible living. Their son, Christian, and I were best friends and went all over Los Angeles together from junior high school until we were adults. Their daughter, Charlene, was several years ahead of us and attended Howard University in Washington, DC. Christian knew his sister as his protector who guarded him carefully and made sure the bigger boys on the block did not threaten or seek to do him any harm. Christian was more than capable of taking care of himself, but Charlene had a keen sense of obligation to her younger brother. Just as Charlene protected Christian, Dellena was my neighborhood protector.

Next door to the Harpers was the Davidson family. They had a house full of boys and one of the most beautiful girls in the world, their daughter Estelle. Like some of the other boys on the street, the Davidsons played drums and participated in the weekly Friday night ritual of beating bongos late into the night and throughout the weekend. One of their sons, Thomas, spent a lot of time helping me learn about responsibility. He shared his time taking me to places around Compton and Watts. He was like my big brother.

Across the street lived the Tylers. Mr. Tyler also worked for the post office, and Mrs. Tyler led the Sunday school and youth activities at Ajalon Temple of Truth Baptist Church. It was located two blocks from my home and was right around the corner from the Tyler's home. They had three daughters and a son. Like the Harpers, the Tylers were native Angelenos. They moved into Carver Manor and helped form the new community that had been developed almost exclusively for Black families. Friendships formed and neighbors committed to resolving their own futures.

The new housing development promised a better place for their families. They possessed hope for their children and were determined to make Carver Manor a desirable place to live where their own dreams would come true.

Walking past the homes of neighbors caused me to remember a time when front and back doors remained unlocked throughout the night. It was where strangers did not exist. No matter who you were, somebody would welcome you.

Carver Manor was crime-free and secured by the watchful eyes of neighbors who babysat children of working parents, provided food to the sick and elderly, and organized games and activities to entertain everyone.

We had a very competitive Little League organization. My first baseball coach was Mr. Boaz, an avid Los Angeles Dodgers fan, who lived up the street from my home. He spent his time teaching his players how to handle ground balls, throw to first base, and to turn plays at home plate. His love of the game extended to the boys in our community who were learning how to play baseball for the first time in the Little Leagues.

"Bend your knees," Mr. Boaz shouted to the candidates who wanted to play infield. "Always be ready to receive the ball," he instructed. "Don't wait for the ball. Expect the ball and be ready."

Years later, long after our Little League days, Mr. Boaz died under my hands at Hawthorn Hospital (later named Robert F. Kennedy Hospital). He had suffered a heart attack and was in the hospital recovering when another attack hit him. I was working as an orderly in the radiology department and was a member of the STAT team that responded to in-hospital emergencies.

"Code Blue," blared over the hospital's intercom system. I stopped what I was doing and went immediately to the patient's room where the medical emergency occurred. Just a day before, I saw Mr. Boaz in the X-ray department. We chatted briefly. He still had that big grin that warmed people's hearts.

As soon as I entered his room, I began applying chest compressions just the way we were trained in the hospital's CPR classes. He was unconscious and not responding. I looked at a nurse. "Keep pushing," she said. Mr. Boaz became the first of more than twenty medical emergencies in the hospital that I responded to during my two-year tenure there. He did not survive.

Next door to Mr. Boaz's house lived the Landly family. Mrs. Theresa Landly played piano for her church and taught piano lessons in her home. Her son, Marvin, was an outstanding singer who was in great demand throughout Los Angeles. They were the family of Gregory Landly, the first Black member of the Los Angeles City Council. Although estranged, Mr. Landly would come back to our community in unincorporated Los Angeles County and visit his wife and son regularly. He also was a veteran and had served in the United States Army. He rose from being a janitor at Los Angeles City

Hall to serving his district for twenty-seven years on the City Council.

The Johnson family lived on the other side of Mr. Boaz. Although they were at the far end of our street, their daughter, Laura, was my younger sister Angela's best friend. They were classmates and continued their close ties for the rest of their lives, with Angela eventually becoming the godmother of Laura's only son, Bradford.

A father without boys, Mr. Johnson treated me like his surrogate son. He invited me to sports events at the Los Angeles Coliseum to see the Rams play football or to the Sports Arena to watch the Lakers. We always had good seats at the 50-yard line or above center court. Mr. Johnson was a devout Baptist. He only went to games during the week or on Saturday but never on Sunday.

Across the street were some of our other neighbors, including the Bales, Yancy, Dodd, Whitney, and Davidson families. Mr. Davidson was a teacher at Lincoln Elementary School. He taught one of my classes during summer school when I was going into the fifth grade. He had a deep love for children and dedicated his life to preparing us to be academically successful.

"You have to know how to read, write, and do arithmetic as the basic study blocks to make it through junior and high school," he encouraged us. "I know you boys like to play and have fun, but if you don't develop your brains, you're not going to go very far."

The Dodds were the first family on our street to have a swimming pool in their backyard. Their daughter Danielle and I were in the same grade. She had an older sister several years ahead of us. Smart, friendly, and always ready to assist our teachers, Danielle was a good friend and classmate. She lived at the far end of our street next door to the Yancy family and a couple of houses from the Bales family home. There were only girls in those houses without a single boy among them.

LaTonya Bales also was in Angela's class and lived across the street from Laura. LaTonya was one of the best athletes on the street. She played sports better than most of the boys and was not shy about picking up a ball ready to go.

Angela, Laura, LaTonya, and Wilma's sister, Frances, were all the same age and matriculated elementary, junior high, and high school together. They were joined by Linsey Whiteman, our neighbor who lived a couple doors from the Dodds. They formed a powerful team of intelligent, curious, and very capable young women. They were generous and always available to assist our parents and neighbors. Some years later, the next generation of girls would keep the spirit of strong feminism alive on our street. My sister Dellena's daughter, Yolanda, and her best friend, Jeena Yancy, established their lifelong friendship.

Even now, on a quiet street transformed by new neighbors and years of undesirable intruders, tranquility had redeemed some of the lost glory and glow that had once been the identifying hallmark of Carver Manor in Hollywatts. Every step beneath the soles of my shoes touched old earth as I walked along our street.

Mothers and fathers, brothers and sisters, friends and neighbors created for themselves a reality that prevented a subterranean germ from seeping like foul sewage into homes and flooding them with unwanted influences. Names, faces, and dusty memories of times past erupted into a panorama of our promised land now long lost and transformed into purgatory.

Our community has produced scholars and outstanding athletes. Then, the shift devastated parts of our piece of heaven on earth. Replaced by hell and its minions, the cemeteries began to fill up without room for any more bodies. Tears of pain flowed and flooded from house to house. Instead of books and backpacks toted to school, little men too young to drive became couriers of drugs and guns that became pervasive. Weapons and ammunition destroyed lives and transformed our neighborhood into the hood. The damnable shame is that the demonic plot was replicated across America with predicable outcomes.

A new industry emerged, labeled the "prison pipeline." Children were transformed into social monsters who feared no evil. In fact, too many embraced the deadly traps that reduced their numbers and eliminated them from becoming fully equipped and prepared as social and professional competitors. Instead of seeking upward mobility and the acumen to be competitive in America's corporate structures, kids in Hollywatts became prime candidates for prison cells and wounded victims of the prison-industrial complex. The epicenter of that satanic scheme was rooted in Hollywatts and replicated across Black America. Urban and rural America became saturated with the scent of death.

I remembered my last conversation with Mr. Davidson. I was an adult working as a newscaster in Seattle. He had been in the school district for more than twenty years.

"I don't know how much longer I can stand teaching anymore," he explained to me. "They won't let me teach—I mean *really* teach my students. They just want me to teach to tests and not really prepare my students to actually learn." His voice was strong, but his soul was broken. "They want us to dummy down our students, and I can't take it. I can't do that!" he exclaimed.

Mr. Davidson wasn't just a teacher going to a job. He was an educator serving the children in our neighborhood. His home was three blocks from Lincoln. He loved his students, and he loved teaching. He was our neighbor, our teacher, and our advocate to save the future of children.

Peering at my street now caused me to remember the cheery voices of children laughing and shouting with uncontrollable excitement.

Christmas morning was the happiest, most exciting day of the year. Kids would come out of their homes early to ride their new bicycles or put on a pair of their brand-new roller skates. We played "crack-the-whip" as we lined up, held hands, and skated up and down the street. As fearless children, we had a single goal to skate as fast as possible and then sling the last skater and propel forward. We were too busy having fun to consider the potential danger of the stunt. Our parents were inside our homes preparing breakfast and using telephones to call families and friends all over town and across the country. It was an annual ritual that had not been compromised or changed. Christmas on the street where I lived was a child's delight as we all played loudly, boldly, and publicly.

Lurking in the background and residing sufficiently in disguise, a new reality was emerging that was unfamiliar. It sent me reeling into a mental tailspin that crushed any notions I may have harbored about some possible happy return home. Any notion of experiencing the familiar ideals of our eternal bliss evaporated in a few short days after my return. The street where I lived had been targeted by demons strategically placed in high-ranking, official offices who were committed to transforming our promised land into purgatory.

Shivers ran up and down my spine as I recalled the dark shadow cast over the carnage that befell my neighborhood. Fathers and mothers watched the future of their children snuffed out as engineers of death strolled amid living enthusiasts and roamed the sidewalks outside our front windows.

The changes on my street unfolded within the expanse of my lifetime and among incredibly good people who thought they had left the worst of life behind in the places from which they escaped. They had lived and known too well the history of centuries old traditions that denied their humanity and punished their personhood. My neighbors were very familiar with brutal assaults on Black people occurring from the Southeast—Virginia, North Carolina, South Carolina, Georgia, and Florida—to the Mid-South of Alabama, Mississippi, Louisiana, Tennessee, Arkansas, Oklahoma, and Texas.

Now, our neighbors had to contend with a national pandemic called racism that had spread across America. Moving west was supposed to provide an escape from cruelty at the hands of law enforcement officers who swore an unofficial but deadly oath to uphold the racist standards of traditions that denied the humanity of Black folks. Our parents truly believed there was hope out west in Southern California where life felt safer and people could live out in the open without the steady fear of white brutality. Suddenly, they were discovering that the landscape of America's racial prejudice was even greater than they imagined.

The foul, smoggy air of Southern California that blocked their view of the Sierra Madre Mountain range was indicative of human violations against Mother Nature and her Indigenous children and newly arrived Black Southern migrants. Acts of evil were not restrained, restricted, or reserved for people deemed unworthy of the notions of "life, liberty, and the pursuit of happiness." Those were not intended or reserved for Native Americans, Mexican Americans, or African Americans. It was the prerogative of European descendants to reserve for themselves the ideals of their wayward ancestors to preserve and protect notions of superiority and their manifest destiny.

Our neighbors possessed an insatiable hunger for tranquility and freedom. Their greatest desires fueled a spirit of hope. They believed religiously in the possibility that each of them could achieve in their newfound promised land what they had been denied in the cities and states where they were born and had left behind. The unacceptable conditions they weathered in their past realities created an undeclared transcontinental movement in search of emancipation that eventually led to their mass exodus. But something unfamiliar, unexpected, and unsuspected invaded their land of promise. It was like a sneaking, slithering serpent uncoiled with piercing eyes in a cool, dark corner, biding its time until it was ready to strike.

Then, without warning and with its fangs revealed, the deadly assault occurred with precision and progressed to develop a determined grip on our unsuspecting neighbors. Those relentless, previously undetected demonic forces followed our neighbors to their promised land.

Between the Pacific and Atlantic Oceans and from Canada to Mexico is a nation that has yet to discover its soul and still refuses to denounce or repent for its sins. Thus, it is doomed to repeat its terror against hospitable people who only wished to pursue life, liberty, and happiness as promised in the deformed Declaration of Independence that set a tone for this country's new white inhabitants.

How can a country fight wars for freedom and create founding documents eloquently drafted and signed by their authors and supporters that are drawn upon a commitment to "Liberty and Justice for all," then turn around and institutionalize systems and structures that deny such ideals for Indigenous peoples, whose cultures and ancient ways of life were almost completely decimated by the new arrivals from Europe?

How can anyone take seriously the pronouncements of liberation when tens of millions of Black Africans were kidnapped, bound in chains, shipped, and forced into slavery by those same proclaimers? Ultimately, those grotesque practices were protected and codified to become the laws of the land. The eloquence of self-proclaimed defenders of freedom became muffled amid the suffering and deadly realities endured by the human cargo destined for enslavement in the "land of the free and the home of the brave." No doubt that incomplete statement requires a more precise exclusion clause.

It strains the human conscience to fathom the decimation of fifty-six million Indigenous people (as estimated by College University of London) over a 300-year period between 1400 and 1700 across the United States and the Western Hemisphere. The hospitality Indigenous hosts extended to sea-weary European sojourners was received with devastating and murderous hostility.

Even worse, the foreign settlers deepened and reinforced their offenses by enacting laws to protect their inhumane practices. They rendered Black people as only three-fifths of a person to solidify their own political control and power, while they also legitimized removal of Indigenous peoples from their homelands and claimed their ancient territories as the rightful, legal statehood of the newly arrived invaders.

The conundrum and contradictions are too blatant to ignore and too gross to comprehend. Yet, the ill-intended behaviors of those early foreign settlers shattered any notions of nobility or honor, as the advancement of violence against people of color spread across the emerging new nation. Despite proclamations and newly crafted documents expressing ideals of civil human conduct, declarative statements of noble ideals were, in actuality, mere words on parchment reserved explicitly for monied property owners who were white, male, and Protestant.

The almost daily occurrences of public lynchings of Black people across the South drove my parents and grandparents, along with many of our neighbors, westward across the country in search of safer places to live without fear. Their determination paved the way for the development of George Washington Carver Manor in Hollywatts. Unfortunately, the strange fruit of dangling black bodies from Southern trees were replaced by daily gun violence that resulted in serious injuries and the deaths of their children in their newly desired promised land.

Like many people on the street where I lived, my family planned their escape from the brutal South. They never suspected their efforts would put them in the unforeseen crosshairs and throes of an unyielding pursuer who kept close watch over their successes and advancements. Their persistent enemies waited patiently until a precise moment when the clutches of Hell possessed the most precious purpose of my family's and our neighbors' exodus.

They did not know their children would become vulnerable targets and their innocence would be corrupted. Our parents had raised their children with a sense of safety, security, and sanity. But the lurking danger rooted and hidden in plain view on the street where I lived changed and redefined our reality. Our parents' promised land began to slip away and gave way to purgatory.

It was impossible for me to imagine the radical transitions, changes, or metamorphosis that had transformed our tranquil community into a place where neighbors secured their homes and maintained a watchful eye on strangers and familiar faces. An air of caution and suspicion prevailed where open friendliness had once pulsated from house to house and around every corner. That was no longer evident, and the shifts were undeniable.

NIGHT MUFFINS

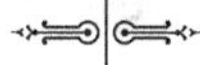

Children in the Streets
Late at Night
Afraid to Go Home
Take Their Chances and Fight
Molested and Raped
Unprotected and Scared
Home Is on Elm Street
No Sanity There
Children Are Wandering
Looking for Love
Macho and Tough
Veneer Mask and Glove
Into the Night
They Stray and Play
Hiding Their Feelings
While Praying for Day

Eleven

The urban struggle for dignity, respect, and human recognition across America by Black folk forged a disruption of domestic tranquility. Three years after the social eruption in Watts, the assassination of Dr. Martin Luther King, Jr. at the Lorraine Motel in Memphis ignited a surge of violence across America. Death was rampant as a rash of deep pain mixed with disillusion created a toxic concoction exploded in the streets.

The year 1968 was filled with gloom, doom, and domestic disorder. Across the Pacific Ocean in Southeast Asia, the war in Vietnam raged and escalated.

Body bags bearing the names of our neighbors continued to arrive in our community more numerously. Young men who had only recently graduated from Centennial High School were returning in fragments of their once-strong physiques. Names so familiar and personalities who once had produced so much laughter came back home wounded or lifeless.

Among those "fortunate" veterans who survived the battles in the fields and rice paddies of Vietnam were faces we once knew. Some returned home without the clarity of healthy minds and with piercing wounds in their souls. Our neighbors' sons followed in the footsteps of our own fathers who had valiantly served the country they dared to call their own during World War II and the Korean War. Now, their sons were returning home from battlefields. They walked into their homes, turned around, and walked back out. They found refuge on street corners with their own unresolved aches inflicted on them in a distant land for reasons still debated in the highest echelons of the American government. The war-weary sons came home in search of sanctuary and sanity. They came back searching for love and a depth of understanding. They sought our promised land to soothe and heal their bodies, minds, and souls.

They came home to live the promises of their fathers and mothers. They came home with long suffering hope of finding and reclaiming the more tranquil life they had left and constantly remembered. Our community was no longer the promised land it had been before they were drafted and sent to Vietnam. They wanted to be reassured their families and their peaceful community had remained untouched and preserved for them. Yet, too often, the survivors of the war in Vietnam came back broken, wounded, and addicted. Their survival was tempered by the new reality they encountered amid transformation. They came home during the emergence of purgatory.

I, too, had been away from home and away from our promised land. My career as a news reporter expanded me in some ways and yet separated me profoundly from unfolding events that captured the attention of children and youth that dragged them into another, much deadlier, world.

The person who interrupted any notions I may have harbored about avoiding the changes evident before my eyes was Byron Tippins. Byron was one of the most brilliant and observant members of our neighborhood. He lived three blocks from my family's home. We had been journalism students together in junior high school in the ninth grade. Mrs. Thelma Harris's journalism class was reserved only for students on the principal's honor roll. Byron was smart, articulate, and a great writer. He also was a very serious person.

We had competed for student body president both in junior and senior high schools. Byron was the sharpest dressed male student at both Willowbrook Junior High and Centennial High School. He was a perfectionist of the first order.

Byron was elected president at Willowbrook. Three years later, I won the office the first semester of our senior year at Centennial. He followed my administration as student body president the second semester.

After graduating from college in the Pacific Northwest, Byron went to law school. During one of my return trips homes, I dropped by his house to see him while he was working in the office of the Los Angeles County District Attorney.

A prosecuting attorney, Byron had only begun his career when he jarred me with news too cruel and demonic for me to fully comprehend. His precise use of words during our sidewalk conversation haunted every part of my body, mind, and soul.

The story he related to me seven years after we had graduated high school was way beyond anything I could have imagined or predicted occurring on the streets in our community. He shocked my nerves and pained my heart with his fervent concern about what was taking place in our neighborhood. It was too remarkably evil for me to easily believe or comprehend.

"You're a news reporter, aren't you?" Byron asked rhetorically. "Why don't you report what is going on here in our neighborhood?" His demand rolled off his tongue with the cadence and tone of a prosecutor.

I mentally and physically took a step back. It was not a mere question. It sounded and felt like an accusation in a court of law before a judge and jury.

"What do you mean?" I asked. "What's going on?"

"Guns," he replied with dead seriousness. "They are putting guns into the hands of children."

"Guns?" I blurted. "What are you talking about?"

"They're putting guns in the hands of our children outside schools, in parks, and at the Foster Freeze right next to Willowbrook Junior High," he continued. "They're handing them out from the trunks of cars and giving them to kids. Real guns," Byron added. "These aren't toys, but the kids are playing with them and using them like toys. Children are getting killed."

I knew a lot had changed in Carver Manor, but I did not know anything about children obtaining guns from sources who came into our neighborhood from outside our community.

"What are you talking about? That's crazy," I retorted.

"It is crazy, and it's really happening." Byron was clearly angry. "Tell that story." His demeanor was straight forward and filled with passion.

My occupation and return to the scene of forbidden crimes made me feel I was party to the scandalous deeds that plagued and endangered families, children, and the people who lived in Hollywatts.

I had been away from our neighborhood almost seven years after we graduated high school. I had left California and was following opportunities to advance my career when Byron and I had our sidewalk conversation. Then, I was living in Seattle, Washington.

The Pacific Northwest had its own issues about Native Americans and Black folk, but it was very different from the hardscrabble existence pervading the streets of Compton and in South Central Los Angeles. Of course, there were incidents of violence and drug-induced clashes and overdoses in the Central District and other neighborhoods in Seattle, but it was different from what Byron had described.

The intentional delivery of handguns given to elementary school children in parks, playgrounds, and nearby hamburger stands next to our junior high school had not fully manifested on many of the streets in Los Angeles—at least not at a noticeable pace. But in Hollywatts, things were becoming very different, and the devastation on the streets where I had lived rivaled the arrival of body bags coming home from Vietnam.

Compton, South Central Los Angeles, and the streets where we lived in Hollywatts became ground zero for the evolution of gang warfare in the last quarter of the twentieth century. Two gangs, called the Crips and the Bloods, were formed in our neighborhood. They divided our community into war zones based on their separate and distinctive colors of blue and red. The Bloods wear red, and the Crips wear blue.

Critically disturbing was the fact that the gangs were organized near the school district's dividing line between Compton High School and Centennial High School. Centennial's school colors are red and white, while the color of Compton High School is blue.

The gangs began to target primarily young boys and recruited them into "street families" that provided a loose semblance of protection and some financial benefits. Young women and little girls were also recruited and lured into the gangs. Eventually, they accelerated and elevated from ragtag rivalries into national, fully militarized organizations.

When mothers and fathers left their homes for work every day, too many of their children were diverted while walking to school. Instead of books, toys, and sports equipment, the children were handed real guns with live ammunition to play with and aim at each other.

There was something deeply planted that took root in the sinister scheme that invaded and transformed our land of promise into an impending purgatory. The colors of the two rival high schools in Compton, California, became drenched in the evil crafting of gang warfare. Those colors began to signify gang territories and were no longer worn to represent the two local citadels of education. The redefinition of school colors worn by children created the differentiation between life and death.

The dissemination of handguns was soon accompanied by the advent of heroin and later crack cocaine on our streets and in our homes. The actual, substantive content mixed in those drugs was not scientifically or medically determined. They were labeled and sold by the familiar terms that they supposedly represented to the buyers and sellers. But, in fact, their actual content was not named or known.

Were those substances actually what they were called on the streets? Too often they were not. In fact, the drugs distributed on the streets where I lived were commonly laced with any number of elements, including talcum powder and rat poisoning. The buyers made their purchases without knowing what was being passed around and sold to them. The death rate of drug overdoses and fatal gunshot wounds soared stratospherically. Children and youth were the primary but not exclusive targets of Satan's scandalous scheme.

Drugs and guns were intentionally placed into the hands of children and youth. In fact, the demonic concoction rapidly replaced baseballs and mitts, basketballs and tennis shoes, and books and homework among the intended recipients. The children were the primary targets.

Block by block, communities were transformed into local battlefields, as turfs and territories were established according to the representative color. Former classmates and teammates began to be identified by their new colorized street families rather than their previous common commitment to excel as scholars and athletes.

The Bloods wearing red were deadly enemies of the Crips in blue. No matter the actual blood ties that bonded biological families, the theology of combat overwhelmed the familial lineages that brought gang warriors into the world. The toxic combustion of drugs, guns, gangs, and fast money mastered the minds and induced the bodies and souls of children and youth on the street where I lived. The streets of our promised land became littered with young bodies who fought the gang wars in defense of their newfound families. The wrong color on the block was sufficient to shoot and kill without malice, question, or cause.

Simply because some stupid fool had dared to wear "blue" in the world of "red" cost a life. Failure to adhere to the manufactured rules of the streets was enough to eliminate the "threat" that was so obvious and immediate. Thus, President John F. Kennedy was prophetic when he intoned, "The living will envy the dead." Then, he spoke of nuclear war. Now, on the street where I lived, it was gang warfare that produced the long list of casualties.

Innocent people don't always see danger lurking in the crevices of their neighborhoods or even in the dens and bedrooms of their homes. Evil has a way of creeping into a place where hospitality was once served, expectedly and anticipated without reservation. That is the predicate of evil's seductive nature.

Unfortunately, notice of evil's presence went undetected on the street where I lived until its destructive claws had penetrated and captured the hearts, souls, and lives of formerly innocent, healthy neighbors, including children.

The evidence of extreme harm was revealed in the drug-crazed zombies who stumbled slowly down the streets where I lived. The desperate craving for another hit of the substance that transformed individual lives and methodically destroyed neighborhoods spread like an unvaccinated victim roaming openly and without regard of advancing the infectious virus.

The absence of medical resources to stem the tide of substance abuse devolved into a criminal action for which there was no substantial, available response. The 9-1-1 call in an emergency was received by law enforcement personnel who were more than adequately trained to put down dangerous situations but who lacked the personal desire, knowledge, or skill sets required to assist a victim of systemic cruelty rooted in a history punctuated with exploitation and abuse.

The promise of a better life for the families of World War II, Korea, or Vietnam war veterans was systematically converted into a devilish nightmare. They fought for their country but returned home to a wasteland littered with family members, neighbors, and school-aged children drifting in a sea of woe. The ritualized drumming on Friday afternoons was silenced. The beat of a heartless plot created to destroy dreams took its place, pounding steadily until the intoxication of fear saturated the street where I lived.

How could anyone defend against an enemy that, in a concocted desire to redesign and redefine a people, collectively fractured every institution formed to build a safer future for those people? Walled within the tragedies of systemic assaults was the compounded fracturing of families and communities. The bonus of such a scheme was to label and criminalize innocent, naïve youth who were previously unprepared for such an invasion. Blaming the victims and restricting access to recovery only furthered a national movement that swept across neighborhoods from across the nation. In retrospect, the network of death became a pattern repeated with predictable outcomes. Thus, the journey from our promised land to purgatory was a direct implication associated with the high cost of the successful Civil Rights Movement.

"My country 'tis of thee, sweet land of liberty, of thee I sing," offers a pristine deception of "truth, justice, and the American way," as echoed in the make-believe cartoon character of Superman. Oh, how we wished, hoped, and prayed the lyrics of "America" would ring true as the actual reflection of real life in our promised land. We stood tall before the flag and pledged our allegiance to a country that repeatedly denied our humanity, dwarfed our dreams, and incarcerated our bodies.

The calculation, profiteering, and tactical corrosion of communities of color may have drained our determination, but it did not deter our destiny. Divine intervention restores the original purpose that preceded the arrival of those latecomers who imposed their dastardly designs and intentions to steal the land and extinguish the people who resided here for thousands of years. Even as the welcoming parties had previously received explorers, merchants, and those who shared the bounty of Mother Earth, there was an expectation that dreams would come true. An expectation that hopes would be fulfilled in line with the continued peaceful co-existence among diverse humans without the demonic passion for greed and exclusive, race-defined conspiracy.

One hundred years after rifles and alcohol were imposed on Indigenous people in a national enterprise to occupy, claim, and control the broad lands from the Atlantic Ocean to the Pacific Ocean and from the north border of Canada to the south border of Mexico, there came a second wave of death plots. The playbook of the late twentieth century reads like a rehashed and updated version of the mass invasion and genocide of American Indians. From rifles to handguns and from alcohol to drugs, the playbook was updated with the predictable results: drugs and weapons falling into the hands of children and youth, a reduction of legitimate job opportunities, the advancement of a culture of crime, and the saturation in neighborhoods of color with hopelessness. Then, provide buyers with deadly, mind-numbing substances, recruit sellers, and let the death parties begin.

The death plots were effectively designed to advance a culture of violence and criminality to promote and justify the emergence of a "prison pipeline" that was skillfully constructed. Through a perverse assault on creativity and artistry, lyrics were written, and seductive rhythms were punctuated that lured young people to the doorsteps of Satan's den. Thus, the advancement of the prison-industrial complex achieved its goal of making mass incarceration and imprisonment a desired destination for those whose dreams were demolished and left abandoned.

The coup d'état was effectively achieved by limiting opportunities for skills training and meaningful employment. Access to quality education and proper preparation for competitive positions were substantially reduced or eliminated in academic environments and school campuses became targets of stealth villains. As a result, hope was more than significantly reduced and sidetracked to shield the true culprits. The proven and familiar convenience of blaming victims and assigning poverty, shiftlessness, and other fabricated determinants was reinforced. But these ideas formulated the reallocation and reduction of public resources from housing, health services, jobs, and the basic needs of individuals, families, and communities.

The advancement of this organized, well-conceived orchestration transformed residential areas into "food deserts" and crime-ridden arenas of incorrigible residents. Then, the scheme advanced further with the reallocation of public funds to finance jails, prisons, and law enforcement. Media campaigns were created to project images of residents in the target zones as weak, powerless, afraid, and out of control of their children, families, homes, schools, and communities. The ultimate objective was to send a message that emphasized that "those" people are a bane on society who must be locked up with indeterminate sentences.

It was not a nightmare that dissipated with the rising sun and people awakening to a new day. Rather, it was the reality that saturated my neighborhood and other communities from coast to coast. That diabolical plan was launched in Hollywatts and transformed our neighborhood from the promised land to purgatory.

THE RIDE

The number is enormous
More than the sand
Killing us wholesale
A child, a woman, a man
A thousand at a time
Ain't it all grand
Too young to know life
Too old to remember
Everybody's getting it
A gun, some stuff, a knife
One way or the other
It's your turn to rot
Believing the government
Thinking it's all good
Rocks in the cradle
Death in the hood
Nobody to save us
A hearse to parade us
Lights out

Slammer shut
Cons turned pros
Filth in the air
No love and no life
Just junk on a dare
Dreams dejected
That is the point
Dealt death's blow
From Satan's own hand
Destroying our people
Missing nary a man
Oh, what a ride

Twelve

Purgatory is that place where the soul awaits its next destination. It is the in-between reality of being and non-being. It is neither here nor there. Yet, an awakening occurs. It is where the awareness of life shifts and true change is inevitable. Purgatory is a stage on which the scenes of past experiences appear and are replayed without interruption.

The soul rests after escaping the embodiment of its human form and reveals the person's innermost thoughts and feelings. The soul finally comes forward beyond the decayed physical structure that limited its true freedom that the afterlife provides. Purgatory allows the soul its full expression without repression. The dreams of a lifetime dive into reality and emerge triumphantly with all the hopes and desires that were trapped within the mortal crust of the human body.

Indeed, purgatory is that place between heaven and hell off the map of places foreign and domestic. It is that destination preachers refuse to preach to congregations and poets fail to accurately pen.

After the foul stench of death and the rotten corpse erases the memory of those whose lives go unrecorded in the annals of human experiences, purgatory welcomes their new existence with a banquet prepared upon their arrival. Their living was not in vain. The violence that invaded our promised land is no longer the epithet that defines the purpose and outcome of our lives. The truth of our demise is brought forward with evidence of the planned destruction of everything previously dreamt, prepared, accorded, and unrewarded. No. Oh, no! Our living is not in vain.

The barbaric invaders who swore an oath to transform our promised land into purgatory on Earth now must face the eternal consequences they never imagined while they schemed to snatch the dreams of noble, faithful, decent women and men who successfully planned and executed their escape from racist hell holes across the Great American Plains.

Everything is revealed with judgment pending for the perpetrators who defied God, denied truth, and persistently imposed their demonic will on innocent souls who longed to live a life of promise.

The names of every victim of America's triumphal charade are called aloud as the parade of witnesses shout out and speak up bearing testimony to the actual truth. "Say their names!" is the long-lasting chant for every person who was lynched, burned out, shut out, shot down, forced to spreadeagle on sidewalls, pushed up against stone-cold walls, shoved with clubs for daring to demand "liberty and justice for all." "Say their names!" is recited again and again and again.

"Say it loud: I'm Black and I'm proud!" screamed the youthful survivors of the Civil Rights era who refused to be silent by an order of the court. Those kangaroo courts set up to protect the guilty and charge the innocent with crimes conceived by their accusers whose sole purpose was to suppress the truth and subject the innocent to the whims of heartless, lifeless brutes.

"Say their names!"

The faceless, forgotten masses are standing in front of their assailants bearing the scars of premature death and dashed dreams.

"We hold these truths to be self-evident," spills out of crooked mouths with Southern drawls, East Coast snobbery, Midwest twang, and West Coast arrogance. Their hatred clings to the final beats of their merciless souls and smothers their choking breath.

Innocent children and eyewitnesses present the true, uncontested evidence of crimes against humanity as they reveal the demonic complicity in the killing fields of America. The cries of the original peoples who are inappropriately called Indians and other monikers that misrepresent their identity and their ties to these vast lands have yet to be fully heard, and their tears have yet to dry. Where is their redemption? Where is their compensation? Who can resurrect their dead?

Who calls out the woes of Black people who were rendered less than fully human with the convenient political assignment of being legally counted as three-fifths a person, each, to bolster the voting count among Southern racists whose very livelihood depended on their desperate need for misrepresentation? No, not their representation. No, not their reparations. No, not their compensation. No, not their presence in the sight of the High Court that deemed Black people had no rights.

"We hold these truths," is festered with engraved lies that fly in the face of those who penned such terms and transformed each verse into an exaggerated bale of falsely constructed ideals. There can be no truth when the premise is saturated with protected regulations and legal practices that reduce and deny human persons the right to breathe and freely exercise their full existence.

The new frontier is littered with decay and disease brought forth from death in the blood-soaked fields where innocent souls reside, buried beneath the earth. That wasteland is such a deadly distance from where there is any hope of ever arriving at such a destination. Instead, they are trapped in the daily reality of hell born of greed and contrition. The suffering of proud, beautiful, powerful, life-loving men, women, and children has yet to cease even in the aftermath of poetic rhetoric and disingenuous legislation that did too little to save the children or brighten the path to a promised land long-awaited but steadily denied.

We can only imagine the significance of escaping the brutal, deadly South and discovering upon arrival in the warmth of the Southern California Sun that they had entered a protracted purgatory. Within the haunting uncertainty of their destination is the perpetually cruel reality our parents and their parents and their parents before them lifted their voices in song to escape. They elevated their prayers while hoping and surrendering their human souls amid the denied promises of liberation and a better way of life that turned bitter with every spoken word of freedom.

The continuing saga of human cargo on the ancient voyages that sailed on the turbulent seas to destinations previously unknown to them has revealed the devilish intent of soulless captors who rewarded themselves with lands stolen from ancient, Indigenous residents and by snatching the desperate dreams of freedom among their captives. We dare not believe the end is near, or we risk falling into the mire of deterred hopes and denied desires for the fulfillment of dreams hoped for and the evidence of things not seen. Yet, there remains the triumphant cheer, "Still I Rise" so beautifully and faithfully penned by Sister Maya Angelou.

Truly, our faith is the source that fuels our journey. Our faith determines our ability to endure beyond the limits of human capacity. It is our faith that mysteriously propels us through and beyond the clutches of satanic beings who masquerade as human but whose deadly souls blatantly reveal the essence of their ungodly cause and existence. Yet, the faith of our fathers and mothers still strives and revives our souls. The promised land lies straight ahead. On the eve of his murder and in his final analysis, the Reverend Dr. Martin Luther King, Jr. prophesized, "I may not get there with you. But we, as a people, will get to the promised land."

FOR YOU, FOR ALL

You gave me your body
Your brains and your trust
A sanctuary in a world
Made from dust
Together we forged
Against all odds
To become family
In the eyes of God
You restored my joy
You healed my soul
Your love is the ground
From which I'm born

Acknowledgments

This story began with my parents, Arthur Lawrence Cribbs and Hattie Dellena Morrison Cribbs, whose love produced three children: Dellena Camille Cribbs Floyd, Angela Bessie Cribbs Urrutia, and me, in a household where love never waned. Our grandmother, Bessie Bowen Gordon, along with our godparents—Herman and Camille Murphy, Willie and Fannie Thomas, and Anna Butler—were a formidable force who imbued us with their values. Our childhood pastor, the Rev. Dr. George W. Bell, along with our neighbors, the Reverend and Mrs. Earl and Earlene Autry and the Reverend and Mrs. E. Boyd and Pearl Esthers, instilled awe of the mystery that bonded us into woven cloth.

Our parents and neighbors from Memphis, Tennessee, formed a network of sojourners who escaped the perverted misinterpretation of "Southern Hospitality" that threatened Black folk who dared to believe their own lives were more valuable than the norms that rendered them worthless. Zollie and Ruby Johnson joined the migration and produced Wanda, Zooey, and Zeke. Together, our transplanted families formed an unbreakable bond of friendship.

Along the way of writing this story, one person constantly asked, "How is the book coming?" Thank you, Lela Bohannon, for your steady voice of encouragement. Also, I am extremely grateful to Brian Bodager, the Executive Director and President of the United Church of Christ Pension Boards, who read the early manuscript and encouraged me to write on.

When I was seventeen years old and merely two days out of high school, I joined a team of ten young people who lived and worked together in the West San Gabriel Valley, a suburb of Los Angeles. There, the Rev. Roy Smith entered my life and set me on a course that grounded the transformation and expansion of my political, theological, and emerging social justice views. Roy challenged my assumptions and urged me to read broadly. I am thankful to Roy for coming into my life and introducing me to the United Church of Christ.

The American Friends Service Committee sponsored that summer project where I met Gordon Dalbey, who had been in the Peace Corps in Nigeria. A prolific writer, Gordon became a source of inspiration as we both became ordained ministers in the United Church of Christ.

The Rev. Bill Moremen, pastor of Western Knoll Congregational United Church of Christ, his wife, Grace, and a young man named Daniel Flores Romero helped to forge my path into the United Church of Christ. Dan imprinted his legacy before he left Los Angeles to attend college in Washington, DC. Dan and I became colleagues in the UCC, and we traveled around the world.

The Rev. Dr. James Hester Hargett and Dr. Louilyn Funderburk Hargett, my spiritual guardians, accelerated my racial awareness and sense of responsibility to our ancestors and generations yet to be born. I am deeply indebted to them for deepening my racial awareness.

Ms. Enaid Savage literally walked into my life in the very early stages of imagining this autobiographical novel. She provided a safe and quiet haven to allow the flow of memory to emerge onto these pages.

This project would not have left the deeper recesses of memory without the early encouragement of my longtime childhood friend and long-distance traveling companion, George Christopher Harpole, III. Chris planted the seeds and nurtured the idea of telling a story about the people and events on the street where we lived. Thank you, Chris, for believing in the possibility of bringing together multiple stories shared by the common lot of our neighbors whose husbands, fathers, and sons went away and fought wars before returning home to their wives, mothers, daughters, and sons in search of a safe place to raise and provide for their families.

I am grateful to Arlene Smith, Dorothy Reed, Alexis Miles, Charles Robinson, and Glenn and Donna Davis. You are the wind beneath my wings who kept me sailing through the gusts and shifts that moved this venture onward. And, to my global accompanist and traveling companion, Calvin Roberts, thank you for believing in the possibility of completing this project every step of the way.

Mike Goodkind, my roommate and fellow news reporter in Reno, read the early rough draft and provided insights into expanding personal stories.

The title of this project was the brainchild of my brother and college roommate, Wesley James Smith. Early in our friendship, I referred to my neighborhood as "Hollywatts, a suburb in the ghetto." Wesley suggested I put that creative moniker right up front.

Throughout this whole process, my family encouraged me. Eternal gratitude to my children: Equenia Petrice Cribbs Bohn, Kiel Jalal and Eniah Handy, Mika Delange Cribbs, Camille Angela Cribbs, and Arthur Ryoma Cribbs; my grandchildren, Jacob Joshua Villa, Kamilah Handy, Kiel and Khalilah Handy; my nieces and nephews

Yolanda and Kenneth Shann, Kianna Shann, Kashay Shann, Britney Mathieu, Ashani Mendis and Kenny Shann; Odell and Loretta Mathieu, James and Odessa Robinson, Reginald Stepter, Linda Handy, and Sal and Sharon Menendez.

About the Author

Arthur Lawrence Cribbs, Jr. grew up in unincorporated Los Angeles County in a post–World War II residential community that was developed intentionally for African American veterans and their families. His father and mother gained their livelihood as a janitor at the Los Angeles County General Hospital and on the rollout line at McDonnell Douglas Aircraft factory in Santa Monica, California. Following in his elder sister's footsteps, Arthur joined the newspaper staff at Willowbrook Junior High School in Compton, California, in the ninth grade. Upon graduating from Centennial High School in Compton, he received a college scholarship in journalism. His career as a radio and television newscaster allowed him to work in cities around the country. In addition to becoming a journalist early in his life, he also became a minister and served as the assistant pastor to his father, who helped to start churches throughout Southern California. He has two sisters, three daughters, two sons, two granddaughters, and two grandsons.